Let's Get Primitive

Let's Get Primitive

The Urban Girl's Guide to Camping

Heather Menicucci

Illustrations by Susie Ghahremani

TEN SPEED PRESS
Berkeley | Toronto

The supplies, tips, and advice in *Let's Get Primitive* are for moderate trips in warmer weather. If you'd like to brave winter camping, traipse through the Grand Canyon for two weeks, or forge into grizzly bear territory, please consult the experts who always do everything by the book.

Copyright © 2007 by Heather Menicucci
Illustrations © 2007 by Susie Ghahremani

1🔄

Ten Speed Press
PO Box 7123
Berkeley, California 94707
www.tenspeed.com

Distributed in Australia by Simon and Schuster Australia, in Canada by Ten Speed Press Canada, in New Zealand by Southern Publishers Group, in South Africa by Real Books, and in the United Kingdom and Europe by Publishers Group UK.

Cover and text design by Chloe Rawlins
Illustrations by Susie Ghahremani

Library of Congress Cataloging-in-Publication Data
Menicucci, Heather.
  Let's get primitive : the urban girl's guide to camping / Heather Menicucci.
    p. cm.
  Summary: "A practical guide to camping basics for urban women that features information on planning, packing, setting up camp, campfire cooking, and camp activities, plus how-to tips and crafts"—Provided by publisher.
  Includes index.
  ISBN-13: 978-1-58008-788-9
  ISBN-10: 1-58008-788-4
  1. Camping—Handbooks, manuals, etc. 2. Outdoor recreation for women. I. Title.
  GV191.7M45 2007
  796.54'082—dc22
                            2006034393

Printed in the United States of America
First printing, 2007

1 2 3 4 5 6 7 8 9 10 — 11 10 09 08 07

*For my mom and dad, who in their own
unique and important ways make sure
my campfire never goes out.*

*And for my special scout, Charlie,
who carefully tends it every day.*

Contents

LEAVING KITTENISH BEHIND FOR WILDCAT
Why I camp, and why all smart, busy, modern, thrifty,
crafty, fashionable, and fabulous urban gals should too.

TRACKING SEA TURTLES AND SPYING WOODPECKERS
What is camping, anyway? Where do campers camp?
And how to plan a first campy excursion.

SQUIRRELING AWAY THE NUTS (AND BOLTS)
The gear essentials, where to get them, and how to use them.

MAKE LIKE A SNAIL
What to bring, what to leave home, and how to squeeze it
all into a backpack.

Acknowledgments

I have an impulse to thank everyone. I know I'm not alone. Lots of acknowledgment pages are the result of a long inner struggle over who to thank. Is there anything wrong with wanting to thank everyone? I believe this all happened like a Rube Goldberg machine, through a series of people and occurrences that aligned in a certain perfect way. In that case, thank you to old friends, new friends, lost pen pals, random acquaintances, former bosses, current bosses, the lady I bumped into at the bookstore, and the guy who pumped my gas with a smile. Thank you everyone!

More specifically, the greatest thanks to my mom and dad, Liz, Phil, Grandma Cranberry, and my whole big extended family, who've always fed me, hugged me, pinched me, teased me, supported me, and cheered me on. I can't imagine where I would be without your big, robust love.

And to Charlie Abriel for sharing his disarming scouting skills, but much more, for his unfailing ability to make me smile and occasional willingness to let me pout. Your superpowers make it easy to write, dance, concoct, imagine, sing, leap, even live.

Super-duper thanks to Laura Wilson for magically making time when there wasn't any, to be my vital second set of eyes. Your criticism, ideas, and suggestions made me work harder and, without a doubt, made this book better. Designer, horticulturist, lounge singer, copy editor—is there anything you can't do?

And to all the brave Glorious Ladies of Kentucky—Rachel Poritz, Jennifer Schwinn, and Laura Wilson—for embracing last-minute adventure and heading down south in the middle of the night in a borrowed car. (And thanks to Brian for the car!) Our trip constantly reminds me what this book is all about.

Special thanks to the Agency Group, Marc Gerald, and especially Caroline Greeven, for seeing a whole big book in my little article and then convincing me I could pull it off. Your guidance was essential to the birth of this book.

Extra special thanks to everyone at Ten Speed Press, but most of all to my editor, Julie Bennett, who surprised me by being not only someone I like to have dinner with but also a person I completely trusted to make this book the best it could be. Your ideas and suggestions on everything from content to art were right on. I also can't possibly leave out Kristi Hein, a fellow camper and nature gal, whose insightful and thorough copyedit helped put the shine on this book and saved me from looking like a fool on a few occasions.

Thanks to Debbie Stoller and the ladies at *BUST* for welcoming girly camping into their amazing magazine and giving me my first real taste of publishing.

And to Tsia Carson and all the folks at supernaturale.com

who first inspired me to share my love of camping with the crafty community.

Thanks to nature and camping lovers everywhere who drive me to keep at this.

And finally to sisters, specifically mine and Charlie's—Samantha and Marisa—who both deserve to see their name in lights but will have to settle for this page for now.

Chapter 1

Leaving Kittenish behind for Wildcat

Why I camp, and why all smart, busy, modern, thrifty, crafty, fashionable, and fabulous urban gals should too.

I'm no longer a stranger to the backcountry, but wandering in the forest is not something I frequently do alone. While camping with friends in Georgia, I had no choice but to strike out on my own to escape the painfully catty campsite vibe. Veiled questions and terse answers. Meaningful breathing. Combative silence. I figured I'd better take a hike before my inner bitch came out to play.

I slung my camera around my neck and snuck off during a debate over the evils of butterfly chairs. I followed a stream that, before I realized it, led me to a couple setting up their private sanctuary. I waved and skulked away. I tried to lose myself in photographing the canopy of orange leaves above, exposed tangled tree roots, and minute mushrooms. But I got turned around. I backtracked. I couldn't find any familiar markers. I'd done some investigating away from camp before but never any real hiking by myself. Would I be able to find my way back without screaming for help? Where had I gone wrong? Why hadn't I brought the damn trail map? Even a cigarette would have been a welcome companion, but I'd forgotten those too.

I struggled up to a perch atop a boulder. My rear's need for a helpful push was another pathetic reminder of my solitude. I felt so sorry for myself, I didn't realize I was having one of those fabled moments in which you get so lost in being alone, you don't see you are no longer alone.

Below, a young family was exploring the same rocks that I was too busy being miserable *on* to take any interest *in*. Athletic Dad was up ahead, and Mom lagged behind holding hands with a girl of about six. The ladies were not prepared to rough it— Mom was wearing leather shoes with pointy toes and Daughter wore a yellow sundress. After their walk in the woods they would probably catch a movie and bring home a pizza.

Mom certainly saw me, but she graciously tried not to make eye contact. I looked purposefully at a leaf so they couldn't tell I was lost, but the little girl sensed I was a fool. She stared at me. Her mom pointed out pretty birds, flowers, and pebbles, but still she stared. I tried to discourage her with a tight, stern smile, but it didn't work. I didn't have the wherewithal just then to be dissected by a six-year-old, but I was trapped. If I tried to jump down I might break my camera, my pride, or, worse, my leg.

Mom finally had no choice but to acknowledge the object of her little rude creature's gaze.

"Think you'll be a nature girl someday too?" Mom looked at Daughter, and Daughter looked at me with a sudden shy smile. Then she nodded her head of messy curls like there was no tomorrow.

This is the part of the story where I turn and face the camera. In a husky voice I say something sharp, like, "Ain't no nature girl here. When I was your age, I was playing hopscotch in the middle of the West Side Highway." Seriously, when I was her age I did not play in dirt or even outside on the sidewalk very often. I was an only child who hung out with adults. I liked going to the mall with my grandmother and watching my mother blow-dry her hair. If my ponytail wasn't perfect, there'd be trouble. I hated getting wet. On annual trips to the seashore with my dad, I'd sneak back to our rented house to watch television and eat potato chips in the air conditioning. Forget asking me to do anything physically demanding. In second grade I quit the soccer team after the first game. As a freshman in high school I thought I'd try basketball, and after four games I became the team manager. All along, I never lost my appreciation for the perfect ponytail. Raised on fantasies of being Madonna. Lover of all things vintage. Paranoid checker of caller ID. Cheap Scotch drinker. Abuser of glitter and glue. Just this morning, before I started my hour-long ritual to get ready for work, I drank six cups of freshly ground coffee, checked my three email accounts twice, and spent ten minutes in front of the mirror practicing applying my new $15 tube of Frisky Fuchsia lip gloss. I can't be the flaxen-haired, easy-going, plant-hugging, lithe nature-girl type that looks good without makeup; I dye my hair black.

So how did I end up in a forest conning a little girl and her mom into thinking I was one with nature? Truth is, I love camping. I think it's hysterical that I have an excuse and an opportunity to get dirt on my face. I like looking down and seeing my old pink Converses jump across rocks. Toasting anything over a campfire makes me giggle. I even enjoy being weighed down by a bag filled with everything I need to survive (for a few days). I like both the physical labor and the bragging about enduring the physical labor. I love drinking my morning coffee looking out on a valley of people all going about business as usual. And I do a little jig whenever I get to have a waterfall all to myself.

More than for all these reasons, though, camping is thrilling because it's something I never thought I could do. Camping is my secret trap door between the modern material-girl life and the gritty uncomplicated existence of a mountain mama. Like reading the classics twice, knitting winter scarves for all the kids in your family, learning to cook whatever your mom cooks, and turning up the stereo to dance when no one's around, camping

Nature nurtures. Poets, philosophers, architects, psychologists, and Eastern religions have always praised the restorative effects of nature. Why do you think they pair horses with addicts and crazy people? Somewhere deep inside, we need this nature stuff. We're sorely deprived of the mood-improving negative ions from waterfalls and oceans, the calming effects of tall still trees, and the perspective-inducing struggle of wild animals. In the city, green is too often sacrificed for the convenience of another Dunkin' Donuts. Get out there and get happy. 🐾

is something we all should do on our way to becoming beautiful wrinkly old ladies with knots of long white hair.

After I recovered from the shock, I considered telling that little girl the truth about me—how I was lost and an imposter. Instead, I took her picture. Her face hangs over my desk—a sweet, smiling reminder that a city-bred Italian-American princess can occasionally pull off nature girl.

A Camper Is Born

I don't think I even knew anyone who camped until I was in college. When I was a kid my mom took me to bed-and-breakfasts in any quaint town within driving distance, and my dad rented a more lavish oceanfront condo each year. When I was old enough to pick my own vacations, I yearned to experience the fashion, food, music, and boys of every city, from Los Angeles to London.

On boys. I don't want you to get the cockamamie idea we all need boy scouts to go camping. My scout piqued my camping interest, but I've learned more from doing things on my own. Ladies-only campouts are like girls' bathrooms, shopping sprees, and nights on the couch—absolutely essential to our well-being. This is not to say boys are to be avoided. Boys are funny and cute and give great hugs. You may want to invite them to join your troop. Just know that, contrary to popular belief, this is a not a male-required activity. If you do decide to let the boys join in, you don't have to rely on them to do the dirty work. 🐾

I fell into camping by pure chance. I met a special Boy Scout and found I was fascinated by his stories of skits, sing-alongs, leather crafts, canoe races, plant identification, and toasted marshmallows. I was struck by the camaraderie that seemed to grow from being outdoors, and I longed for my own troop. I interrogated him. I couldn't get enough. His tales unearthed an unexpected childhood fantasy. As a kid I hadn't wanted to be a Girl Scout like my dorky neighbor. I'd preferred to stay inside and tend to my Boy George collages. But somewhere along the way I had developed a secret longing for my merit badge in roughing it.

I decided it was time to pursue this mysterious new experience. And what better occasion than my birthday? With some help from my scouting friend, I set off on my maiden voyage to the backcountry. I traded my favored birthday ritual of tapas and sangria for trail mix and warm tequila. The rest is history, I guess. I haven't spent a birthday within civilized limits in years. I fell in love. I'm hooked. And I am dedicated. Hell,

On scouts. Scouting, like the nuclear family and hot apple pie, is a fascinating throwback to old-fashioned Americana, but the organization also has an unfortunate reputation for antiquated exclusiveness and closed-minded intolerance. Coincidentally, the Scouts have actually been a haven for kids who don't make the in crowd—the geeks. I love that about them, and I can't resist their nifty projects. So in the spirit of revamped vintage, *Let's Get Primitive* will occasionally borrow and adapt some of their traditions. ❧

I'm hell-bent on proving every city girl can rock the backcountry without a mirror, shower, cell phone, deodorant, or even a toilet. *Let's Get Primitive* is my collection of camping experiences turned into makeshift advice and homegrown wisdom and my personal invitation to all city girls to get out there and get dirty. Let's get primitive!

Back to the Caves

Why *let's get primitive* and not *let's go camping*? In part I was inspired by Olivia Newton-John. Substitute *primitive* for *physical*—I think you'll agree it's pretty catchy. More important, the word *camping* conjures up an image of the crunchy-granola crowd, dressed in bland colors, drinking water, and eating gorp. I say we do this our own way. It's a camping revolution and a city girl's devolution.

My first camping trip was an homage to improvisation. That helped make camping more me, more approachable. I'm not an expert. I don't own all the right gear. Skirts, pressed powder, water guns, and wine all make appearances on my packing lists, and I've never worn a fanny pack. I squeal in the presence of bugs, and I love to complain. Still, I camp. A secret: it's easy! I'll walk you through important camping guidelines but also point out which rules are best broken. I'll explain what the heck camping really is and where you can do it. I'll share my tricks—from rolling up an old blanket to use as a sleeping bag to planning the ultimate back-to-reality shower. I'll show you how I spark up a toasty campfire and rig up a shelter for watching the storm. You'll create your own daypack, perfect a recipe for classic camp biscuits, and award your troop with handmade merit badges. This is the camping manual for girls who appreciate crowds, all-night sushi, bike messengers, street vendors, and good public transportation. I hope it inspires you to throw a rooftop sleepover, pee behind a tree, take a minute to watch the birds, or spend a day without switching on the lights, but I won't be satisfied until you pitch your first tent in the backcountry. *Let's Get Primitive* is not just a guide; it's the urban girl's call of the wild.

Why Bother?

There are hundreds of reasons I camp. It's a do-it-yourselfer's delight. You'll perfect all kinds of handy old-school skills, from knot tying to weather predicting. You'll come home bronzed and badass, creative and capable. The looks you get when you say you've returned from a three-day canoe trip will keep you smiling for weeks. Road trips are the best. And being able to pick up at any time and hit the road is even better.

A paper security blanket. I slip a book into my bag anytime I'm headed to a new place. If you've got a book, you've always got a retreat. What should you do with *this* book? Lay it open beside you while you shop online for a tent, practice knots, or pack. Read it cover to cover or skip around. Tuck it into your backpack to use as your field manual. *Let's Get Primitive* is easy on the eyes but ready for a bit of the rough and tumble. ❧

Every six months or so I come down with a case of inertia. The things I like to do are suddenly boring. I'm listless and, worse, cranky about it. Camping is the only cure I've found for this immobility. A weekend of living simply, trading the abstract for the concrete, is a mental jumpstart. Even better, camping is a rare opportunity to take off your costume. Let your hair get frizzy. Transcend your schedule. The utter lack of everything we're accustomed to seriously shakes things up. You'll be inspired to do cartwheels and compose odes to ferns. On your lonely walk to the dreaded cat hole, you may discover butterflies mating. Just when you begin to get sick of the rain, you invent a new game and discover you can draw. There is no shortage of seemingly synchronistic, magical moments in the backcountry. Not to mention that making things out of twigs and then lighting them on fire is fun. Truth is, I wouldn't put myself through weekends without plumbing if camping was anything short of amazing.

Do the math. Is there anything better than vacation? If I could afford to fly to Morocco for one night, I'd fit it into my schedule at least once a month. But until I find that pot of gold, I'm trapped in my financially challenged reality. Enter camping. A night in a backcountry spot usually costs somewhere between $0 and $20. Gear can be borrowed. Supplies scored cheaply. And a bit of pristine turf is probably within two hours of your front door. Become a camper, and you'll always have an escape no matter how low your funds or short your time. 🐾

Get the Gusto

I think I'm in the female minority when I confess that I don't use the Pill. Every time I pop those magic little tablets, I go insane—sudden tears, irrational tempestuousness, scratching, clawing—more so than usual. During one of these stints as chemical hormonal girl, I attempted my second backcountry trip ever. We left three hours later than planned and sat in Friday rush-hour traffic. Thumping bass from passing cars drowned out the bittersweet Mountain Goats, but nothing could mask my intermittent heaving. Five horrific hours later my troop arrived in Fire Island, New York, where we began

Still need convincing? Meet the Glorious Ladies of Kentucky (GLOK for short)—three metropolitan maidens who trekked down south for their first-ever primitive experience. They joined the campaign to light the campfires of city mice everywhere and volunteered to share their trip in the pages of *Let's Get Primitive*. They are sure to inspire with their shocking display of survival skills and their infatuation with all varieties of cheese.

Cue the music. Turn on the spotlight. Wait! I've been wracking my brain for weeks trying to figure out the best way to introduce each glorious lady. I mean, what would do their unique personalities justice on paper? Is it important to know that Jen lists having the freedom to break out in Broadway show tunes as one of her favorite reasons to camp? Or that Laura is the girl I roasted my first (and only) duck with? How about that she's got enviable strawberry blonde hair? Later, when you hear about Rachel climbing a rock, is it integral to know she's a our two-mile trek through burning hot sand. Each time we passed a sign that didn't say "Camp Here," I lost it. Happy families with golf umbrellas and coolers brimming with beer studied the crazy crying camper with curiosity. Something, probably our increasingly gamy scent, attracted a swarm of horseflies. Stings, pinches, and bumps popped up all over our exposed skin. When one bugger bit my lip twice I had to stop short of smacking myself. The chemicals chanted to me, "This is nuts! What are you doing? You should be home on the couch. Heads will roll," and so on. I tore my pack from my shoulders and flung the canteen. Turning to scream at anyone within range, I saw that my campmates were already halfway into the

lawyer who designs jewelry? Most important, you should know these city chicks took to the backcountry and wielded dazzling feral wiles. Also, you might be interested in two other factoids about the girls.

Okay then, on with the introductions. Meeeeet Jennifer! Jennifer's favorite cheese is smoked gouda. And in the movie of her life she would like to be played by Reese Witherspoon. Laura, lover of buffalo mozzarella, hopes Claire Danes isn't busy when production starts. And last but not least, Rachel, big fan of dill havarti, couldn't decide who would pull off her character best, so I picked for her: Selma Blair will be the lead in *The Rachel Story*. As for me, I go gaga for any cheese of the goat variety; and if Christina Ricci turns down the part, I'll be heartbroken. Heading back north with this carload of crazy camping converts made me think anything is possible. I hope they do the same for you. 🐾

ocean. "Hurry!" they yelled just before diving in. I looked at my red, bitten, puffy hands and decided to kill them after a swim. Clothes and all, I ran for it. Like a frosty margarita after

Gateway drugs. Conjure a jones for the wild. Coax out your inner cave woman by taking a few baby steps first. Convince yourself you've just got to have more of the great outdoors. Try these easy local and at-home activities before you take the primitive plunge.

- Bring home the master of the nature documentary, David Attenborough. Rent *Portrait of the Earth, The Life of Birds, Blue Planet*—when you see that old chap trounce around in his little brown kicks you can't help but wish you were right there beside him sniffing out ant hills.

- Craft natural. Any time I turn my lens on greenery I feel like an ace photographer and I get psyched about the wilderness. Take your camera for a walk or get some close-ups of houseplants. Frame fall leaves, cover a box in seashells, press flowers into paper—you may find you're driven to trek into the backcountry for the most unusual art supplies and willing subjects.

- Drive up to inspiration point. Famous scenic drives crisscross America and traverse national parks and forests. Do a quick Internet search; even the names are inspiring—Going-to-the-Sun Road, Artist's Drive, Hell's Canyon Byway. Observing the wild through the car window just might make you want to burst through the glass. 🐾

a crappy day, a starlit hot-tub soak in January, napping in the afternoon, and soft-serve vanilla from the ice cream man, like all the clichés describing bliss—it was awesome.

We emerged from the waves only fifty feet from the camping area. The sweat was gone. The bugs retreated. We prepared a meal of gingery jasmine rice with cashews, and thoughts of murder dissipated. I cried only a few more times the rest of the trip.

No matter how you spell *relief*, I guarantee you'll get some in the backcountry. Camping is good for the works—your works. It has the practically indescribable qualities of things that feel nourishing and good and right.

This is not to say it's all puppies and kittens. Sometimes nature is exasperating and exhausting. Oddly enough, it can be too real. Or too cold, or even too crowded. Sometimes I get out in the great wide open and realize I'd rather be sitting in a poorly decorated, smoky hotel piano bar. That's okay. Au revoir backcountry. Till we meet again. I have no problem walking out of a movie I'm not in the mood to see, and I'm not suggesting camping will satisfy all your needs all the time. I'm just daring you to give it a chance. I triple-dog dare you. From one city chick to another, you should do this. Not doing this would be like going into a karaoke bar with your dream song all picked out and never getting up the gusto to get on the mic and belt your heart out. And don't even try to say you can't sing.

Get Inspired

Your first assignment: daydream. Play "Pin the Tent on the United States Map" and make a list of interesting locales to set up camp. Plan your trip guest list and draft the perfect

Funny fears. Years ago I agreed to housesit for friends living in a gated community in the middle of nowhere. They wooed me with promises of burly security guards. They returned home to find warning notices from their community association. Apparently it's frowned upon to call on the security guards five times in one week to investigate suspicious noises, phantom bears, and killer moths. My friends should have thought of that before they promised me protection from the trees. City folk are notoriously wigged by the woods. Check out these flicks and have a laugh at our sophisticated neurosis—nothing is as scary when it's laughable.

- *Deliverance*—the ultimate freaky story of disturbed rednecks. See this to be in on the joke—friends will inevitably hum the popular tune when they hear you're going camping.

- *Friday the 13th*—what camper can forget Jason or his mommy?

- *Redneck Zombies*—the perfect spoof on urbanites with tents. Invite the whole troop over to see this before you go.

- *Texas Chainsaw Massacre*—a classic rendition of our suspicions about country folk and what they secretly want to do to us. ❧

invitations to entice your fellow city slickers. Christen a blank notebook—your first camping journal. Spill your fears about the rural landscape and confess the urban hassles you'd like to flee. Make your journal as personal as your style of camping. I use a wildlife sticker to kick off every new entry and fabric covered with seagulls to decorate the cover. Use photos, dried leaves, maps, or star charts—anything that inspires you. Date your first entry and watch the camping addiction grow. Your journal is where you'll work on supply lists. Highlight where you've been, remember what you've learned, and fantasize about where you're going. Sketch the shelter you invented or the camping shorts you designed. Bring it along on your trips to record the challenges you conquer; peruse it on rainy days when you need an imaginary escape. Before you know it, your journal will be chock-full of wild tales. Soon you'll be roughing it just like a pro. Well, maybe not a pro, more like a Switchblade Sister with a soft spot for flora and fauna.

🐾 🐾 🐾 🐾 🐾

The next assignment is easy: pick your terrain. There's pristine public land in every state just waiting for you to pitch your tent. Will it be a lush forest or a barren beach? A waterfall or streamside campsite? A rigorous hike to your rendezvous, or a hop, skip, and a jump from the trailhead? From finding great camping locations to setting up a site, chapter 2 is all about planning the perfect trip.

Tracking Sea Turtles and Spying Woodpeckers

What is camping anyway?
Where do campers camp?
And how to plan a first campy excursion.

Every third car cruising the highways of the northeastern coast seems to sport an oval *OBX* sticker. It's an emblem that suggests you've played mini golf and possibly downed tequila shots in an oceanfront cafe on North Carolina's barrier islands, the Outer Banks. The banks are the quintessential vacation destination known to families and fraternities alike, but most Italian Americans from New York don't migrate that far down to go to the beach. We're accustomed to the grime, crowds, and freezing cold water of the infamous New Jersey Shore—and we're told to like it that way.

It wasn't until a few years ago I even knew what OBX meant. Against my better judgment and neurotic nature, I let myself get suckered into someone else's camping trip. From what I'd heard, the Outer Banks were a great place to score shell jewelry but certainly not to camp. As we twisted and turned down boggy rural roads toward the ferry service, I learned we were headed to the lesser-known Core Banks. The crew and passengers of our water passage didn't do much to ease my mind. On one side was an evident lack of dentistry and on the other was the grating disposition that comes with being a high school senior. There was also a herd of suburbanites wrangling errant dogs and children, and four potbellied men with an RV. From a safe distance I cracked open a warm Miller High Life from the stash in my pack and took in the show. When the RV began to ease its way onto the tiny, dinky ferry, my group fell silent.

The wind did an excellent job drowning out the kids' screeches, and after only twenty minutes we reached shore with wild hair and a pleasant beer haze. The teenagers and families scattered toward a cluster of cabins. The men with the RV let some air out of each of their tires and slowly pulled away over the sand. And we tried to get our bearings as we trudged over the dunes. Had we come to the wrong place? Was there even

Delicious deliveries. Bacon, eggs, shrimp, cigarettes—you name it. For a slightly marked-up price, Mack would call in your order, and the next morning it'd be ready for you to pick up at his cabin. Deli meat may not qualify as roughing it, but who's judging? Salami is a special reward for venturing off the beaten path. Unusual, quirky, and sometimes even luxurious perks like this are simply bonuses for those willing to brave unfamiliar territory. ❧

primitive camping on this damn island? Would our camping trip provide quaint entertainment for these tourists all weekend? Then Mack pulled up in an old red pickup. Sometimes there is nothing like a rusty pickup truck to make a city girl weak in the knees. Tan, wrinkled, smiling, and ruggedly handsome, Mack filled us in on everything. The cabins are rented to vacationers. Fishermen, and fisherwomen, often drive loaded RVs over to the other end of the island for prime fishing. And we were welcome to camp anywhere in between. He'd even give us a ride so we could get nice and distanced without the agonizing hike through sand. I like hard work as much as the next girl, but I'm not too proud to take charity. I told him he was a dream come true and tossed my pack into the flatbed.

Turned out Mack was just a happy harbinger. The weather and the water were warm and clear all weekend. Ample driftwood washed ashore to feed our beautiful beach blazes. Conches of storybook proportions greeted us when we emerged from our tents in the morning. REM's "Nightswimming" played in our heads as phosphorescent plankton visited us on our nightly skinny dips. Our fellow ferry riders were barely specks on the horizon. We were shipwrecked sailors minus the scrapes and starvation. Now, when I hear the inevitable tales of the best bars and cutest guys on the Outer Banks, I smirk. To me, *OBX* is a reminder of how camping takes you elsewhere.

Camp Here, There, Almost Everywhere

From the epic to the mundane, natural to supernatural, wet to dry, all kinds of experiences await you and your tent. You will find adventures unattainable within civilized limits, inaccessible by taxis or buses, unimaginable from the familiarity of a rented room, and simply unfathomable surrounded by conveniences and crowds. Up and down the east coast and a little toward the middle I've discovered overgrown fields of orange wildflowers; wise hemlocks in elderly forests; mystical swimming holes; mossy chartreuse gorges; leaves the size of my torso; and friendly wild horses. Like a mosquito, I always seem drawn to water, but next up on my list is the rusty dusty desert. Go west, young woman. Or east, or stay local. The first thing to do is get your hands on a good road atlas. Look for pale patches of green with intriguing names—Cheyenne Mountain, Great Sand Dunes, Bitterroot, Green Ridge. A thorough

Get with the program. Need a trip with an agenda to get your motor running? Devise themed voyages. Take a Yeti Expedition—gentle giant or furry foe? Draw your own conclusions in the wilds of Washington, home to the most reported Bigfoot sightings. Embark on *The X-Files* Extravaganza—reenact Scully and Mulder's nonromance romance in a spot rumored for alien visitation. Journey Back to the Ice Age—visit glacial potholes, those odd depressions left all over the United States when the great melt finally came. Plunge into the cool water and visualize our icy past. ❧

atlas will note federal, state, or even regionally owned land—
forests and parks, preserves and wilderness areas. Rules vary,
but most are open to some form of camping and usually for
a paltry fee, if any. Some privately owned campgrounds may
also be highlighted on your atlas. They offer a different kind of
camping with lots of amenities, usually for a higher fee.

Confused? Let's get a few things straight. When people say
camping, they can mean different things; and worse, there are
lots of names for camping too. There's car camping; trailer camping; tent camping; canoe camping; primitive, dispersed, backcountry, and wilderness camping; backpacking—in some circles
even squatting counts. They all bleed into each other, creating
this big gray blob that somehow usually involves marshmallows.
To simplify, there are two fundamental kinds of camping—
campground or *site camping* and *backcountry* or *primitive camping*. That may be a broad distinction, but it singles out the most
important difference. It's the difference between having a week-
end-long tailgate party and a real adventure in a pristine piece
of secluded wilderness.

Campground Capers and Primitive Pursuits

Many of my friends recall childhood memories of family camping trips in cramped station wagons or, if they were very lucky,
camper vans. Their stories involve some combination of barbe-
cued meat feasts at picnic tables, water sports on lifeguarded
beaches, and groping behind restrooms equipped with hot
showers and flushing toilets. A campground is land divvied up

into neat, flat parcels, arranged and numbered, not much differ-ent from a parking lot, with trees. Some offer gravel ground sites, others paved with some grass (usually heavily treaded grass). Campground camping is the height of camping convenience. It's occasionally referred to as car camping because sometimes you can park right next to your tent. The amenities vary widely, but most grounds offer bathrooms, BBQ grills, garbage cans, and lots of retirees. Some so closely resemble motels they have snack bars, pools, and shuffleboard. Arriving late to the ranger sta-tion one night, I slummed it in a bumpin' county ground filled with teenagers who seemed to be rebelling against camping by dressing like they had been plucked out of a music video. Two

Stalking Tarzan by the glow of headlights. Don't be discour-aged if campgrounds sound like all the wilderness you can handle. A campground trip could be your training wheels. Consider it a practice session before you hop on the slumber-ing stallion within. Campgrounds can be found in federal and state forests and parks and in private grounds. Some are cre-ated in the spirit of wilderness and privacy. The most coveted sites may be nestled among trees or along water and are actu-ally pretty darn serene. Plan early and take your time reading campground reviews, which are readily available online. The best spots are often reserved weeks or months in advance. Campgrounds in forests and parks are much more likely to cater to the Jane in you than the privately owned variety favored by big families. Avoid any grounds offering electricity hookups, and ask about areas reserved for tent camping. One night can cost up to about $40. ❧

boys playing Nintendo right outside my tent serenaded me with blips, beeps, and 8-bit music. Campgrounds are cheap alternatives to a night in a hotel, but they're not the sort of thing that requires inspiration. I figure if there's electricity and roving security guards, you don't really need me cheering you on.

I know I sound like a camping snob. I like candy machines and the smell of chlorine too, but when they're accompanied by room service. In campgrounds the power of the great outdoors is dampened, commercialized, and packaged way too neatly. Primitive, backcountry, dispersed, or wilderness camping is the real deal. Think Hello Kitty versus She-Ra. This kind of camping means hiking to a secluded place within a public land and setting up house on a patch of dirt, grass, moss, leaves, or sand. Pick a trail, park your car, hike, and then pitch your tent. Rough it a lot or a little. Walk for five minutes, three hours, or a whole day. Scout out a spot under the first inviting tree, trek for two days to reach a secret cave, or go till you're tuckered. Most forests and some parks on both the federal and state level allow primitive or dispersed camping. There are varying rules, but usually it's as straightforward as it sounds. Some places designate an area for camping, but most just require you to camp two hundred feet away from trails, water sources, and cliffs.

It's good practice to stick to designated or established campsites. These aren't sites in the campground sense; they're scattered and concealed, rather than arranged. Keep your eyes peeled for a sign—as in square metal with a tent symbol—or an old fire pit (a ring of rocks around a sooty black spot), a tree trunk placed conveniently for sitting, or low rocks arranged as tables or seats. Now call on that inner fort-making child and set up camp.

Sound simple? It can be. Push yourself, or take it easy. Explore the terrain, or sit and ponder. Sing around the campfire till dawn, or catch up on lost sleep. Primitive camping is like an interpretive dance. Will you treat Mother Nature to a graceful pirouette or a monster air-guitar solo?

Foraging through Forests and Prancing around Parks

Forests, both state and national, are the most likely locale for primitive camping opportunities, but this isn't a blanket rule. Some of my favorite spots are in parks. The United States Department of Agriculture Forest Service maintains the national forests. Within their domain there are more than 190 million acres of land, including forests, grasslands, and special wilderness areas. This can get kind of confusing, which is why they maintain an excellent website with detailed information

Only you can give a hoot. The backcountry is where all those familiar one-liners about being a good camper come in. There aren't crews scouring the forest for lost rubber bands that some poor birds might painfully mistake for worms. We must clean up after ourselves. And although it completely stinks, sometimes we must clean up after thoughtless neighbors. ❧

about every kind of land and its uses. You'll also find regulations and downloadable maps there.

State forests are a little harder to characterize because they're maintained by different branches of state services with varying goals. To help sort it out, most have websites too, so you can make sense of where you can camp and where you can't. (When you're ready to get technical, flip to the reference section in the back of this book, where lots of handy links live.) Forest camping is often free, but it can cost up to about $15 for one night. A night in the forest may require a permit but not always. Every national and state forest has different requirements, so double-check on the Internet. And while you're busy playing detective, look up the federal Bureau of Land Management. It maintains even more pieces of public land that are also sometimes open for backcountry camping.

It drives me nuts knowing my dream acre could be just around the corner, and I might never know about it. If being obsessive is one of your flaws too, investigate the government's recreation website (listed with the other links in the back of the book) or check out the Federal Land Atlas at your local library, which includes everything from national forests to Native American preserves. Once you've singled out your spot,

Forest facts. Covering a whopping seventeen million acres, the Tongass National Forest in Alaska is by far America's biggest. The second largest national forest is also in Alaska, and it's only a measly five million. 🐾

it's good practice to call ahead to the ranger office for permit information and current conditions. Want a hard copy? Most libraries keep a decent collection of forest and park directories.

Park refers to many different types of recreation lands, so this designation can be misleading. The National Park Service maintains over eighty million acres, including seashores, lakeshores, cemeteries, and even scenic parkways. Obviously not all are open to campers, so do your homework. Search on their website by state or even by natural feature. Look for parks to suit your fetish for wildflowers, coral reefs, or fossils. Once you've singled out a park, the website is pretty clear on whether primitive camping is allowed. State-managed parks are often set aside for day-use activities—picnics, nature walks, fishing. They also commonly host campgrounds, but some are big enough for backcountry camping. Again, a web search or library run should provide answers to your questions or at least a contact name and number. Primitive camping in a park, on both the national and state level, usually requires a permit and a small fee—generally $20 or less for one night.

To Plod or Not to Plod

My first primitive camping trip was to be a savage birthday spectacular of primal pleasures and feral feats. I wanted to commune with birds, gnaw on beef jerky, and, most important, leap into a lake wearing nothing but my birthday suit. At this stage of my camping career I thought a forest was any patch of trees anywhere. I had no choice but to take the advice of my favorite Boy Scout. And why wouldn't I? He's pitched a tent more times than he can remember. One look at the atlas, and he said the trip was planned.

On a gorgeous summer day we hopped into my car and headed north. At the Finger Lakes National Forest ranger station in New York, a nice woman suggested we head to a pleasant campground one mile back up the road, and I started to get a little suspicious. Maybe I should have questioned our hasty decision sooner; this same skilled scout has also disappeared on three hitchhiking journeys without any inkling of a destination. But I scoffed at the suggestion of a "pleasant campground," and we trudged onward in pursuit of a truly primitive adventure. We drove all around the forest, disappointed by the big road system that intersected it, and unable to find a spot anywhere near potable or even swimmable water. Then, just when I should have been sharing cupcakes with butterflies, I was waiting for a tow truck to pull the car out of the ravine we forged down in our futile search for a damn lake. I must have been in shock because I barely remember finding, hiking to, or setting up our campsite. After the cursing and crying finally stopped, I looked around and saw that it was beautiful. This site had positive vibes and good feng shui. A canopy of trees let in just the right amount of

Park pick. Yellowstone National Park, home to grizzlies, hot springs, and odd geologic formations, is probably America's most famous park. Preserved in 1872, it was also the first. 🐾

sun, and a fortress of bushes made it impossible for others to see us from the trail. There was perfect tree placement for hanging a clothesline and the comfiest rocks my heinie has ever known. Most amazing, a glow-in-the-dark fungus lined the tree roots around our tent, lighting a path in the dark. I did not swim once that weekend, unless you count the downpour that surprised us all day on my birthday. Still, that first trip remains one of my favorites (and a testament to the power of a really good campsite). Was it more special because it was all unexpected folly? Could it have been better if we had done our homework and found a perfect site that also boasted a swimming hole?

When I first learned the meaning of "fly by the seat of your pants" I became extremely paranoid that I was too plodding. I was eleven. Is the adventure in the discovery or is it in the ideal destination? To what lengths should you go to make sure your trip is flawless? When you finally get up the gusto to camp, you want your spot to be as spectacular as the surface of the moon. You want to see the squirrels with the bushiest tails, swim in whirlpools of turquoise water, smell wild jasmine, and sleep on a bed of powdery sand. If I only have time to take four trips a

Stay inside the lines. Coloring worksheets, word puzzles, kitchen science projects—the forest and park websites have creative ideas for getting kids amped about nature. And there's no height limit. Paint owls pink, study ant communities, and play junior ranger in preparation for your first outing. 🐾

year, one will be meticulously planned but the others will likely be more impromptu out of necessity. I might pick a forest, check to make sure primitive camping is permitted, download a map, call the ranger, and go. Other times I start with states I'd like to visit. Then I whittle down to forests and parks based on an analysis of the natural features and past campers' opinions. I visit the library, call friends, consult my horoscope. The whole process can take a month.

There is no secret to planning the perfect trip. Try to be flexible. If flexible isn't in your bag of tricks, the great outdoors is ideal for tantrum throwing.

Follow the Crumbs of Information

The pages of my road atlas, which lists forests and parks within a fifteen-hour drive from home, are dog-eared and worn. Trip planning usually starts with the atlas. An intriguing name or new area grabs me, and then I head to the Internet to search for the official website. If it's a national forest or park there's always a thorough website with clear camping regulations and descriptions of everything from wildlife to weather conditions. State forest and park websites vary; I usually call to confirm the facts. Occasionally it's back to the drawing board because there's storm damage, campfires aren't permitted, or there's not much space designated for primitive camping. But if the description sounds promising, I head to the outdoor magazines to see if they've covered my potential destination. *Backpacker* and

Outside magazines have searchable websites, and some libraries maintain print copies. They offer reviews, roundups, and feature articles on interesting camping spots and trails. Their trail descriptions clue you in on the terrain and often suggest campsites worth visiting. Quick cross-referencing between the magazines and the official website usually points me to a specific area within the forest or park I'm considering. Parks and forests are broken down into areas, formally, or informally by other campers. For example, within Daniel Boone National Forest is Red River Gorge Geological Area, and within that is a particularly wild reserve called Clifty Wilderness. Once I'm thoroughly schooled, I'm ready to sneak into the forums.

Approaching the diehard bandana crowd for their priceless pointers can be intimidating. When I first scrolled through the backpacking forums I felt like a bald guy with a beer gut ogling Goth girls' personals. If they could see the kitten stickers all over my monitor would they send the granola police out for me? Then I'd never find out their juicy secrets about which popular national forest is too crowded, eavesdrop on their needling of each others' camping prowess, or check out the photos of wolfman01 on his Appalachian Trail trek.

Hmmm. Camping raises interesting questions, questions that, engrossed in the rhythm of the busy city, you might not consider. Are you willing to venture forth without a real plan? Can you function without email? Where does your mind drift in near-perfect silence? Who knew camping was so deep? ❧

Camping forums are hands down the best way to get the dirt. They're also great for sharing recipes, trading gear, and catching the camping bug. Look for forums that break things down by state so you don't waste precious sorting time. Scoot ahead to the resources section for some of my favorites. Do a little research before you dive in; it helps to speak the language. Campers talking to other campers assume everyone is in the know. They refer to trail names using initials and talk about areas within a forest rather than using the whole name. Don't worry; the outsider paranoia melts away quickly. You might be instant messaging wolfman01 before you know it. Most campers are helpful and generous even though they'd love to keep their favorite spots all to themselves.

When I really want to be carried away by the tide of information, I head over to the personal homepages referenced in the forums. This is where the most enthusiastically detailed, but occasionally flawed, information lives. I've been to a waterfall database, a hobbyist photographer's portfolio of every arch in a park, and a family's blog explaining the menu for every trip

---

Camping often conjures up thoughts of campfires, but fires aren't always permitted in the backcountry. Wind, weather, damage—there are lots of reasons why fires may be prohibited. Sometimes it's worth forgoing a picturesque fire in the interests of enjoying and preserving a special piece of wilderness. Make sure you know and obey the rules. We don't want to give city girls a bad name. 🐾

they've ever taken. If you enjoy research, indulge. Patience with these websites has led me to secret swimming holes and retro but accurate topographical maps.

Next up is the library or bookstore. Through your research you'll often find a certain guidebook repeatedly referenced. People talk of must-have maps or trail guides; I listen and then I buy. Not every trip requires a nerdy stash of data, but it helps to have a trusty trail guide and map. A guide will estimate how long a trail might take to hike and how hardcore you need to be to climb it and often suggests sweet spots to pitch the tent. And a map will help you plan day excursions from camp, tell you where to park, and point you to valuable water sources. Check the date—an outdated guidebook or map is as helpful as a movie ticket stub.

Last stop on the information trail—the ranger station. Give the rangers a call and run your plans by them. Confirm your information about permits, where to get them, and how much they cost. See if there are any special conditions you should be aware of, and inquire about additional materials, like updated maps. My trip-researching obsession has earned me the job of itinerary planner on more than one occasion. For a close-by

When I sought advice in the forums for the GLOK trip, nostalgic ladies chimed in about their first times, and dads asked if we'd bring their daughters. A lot of campers may not appreciate your Diesel jeans, but they will help you feel at home in their Gore-Tex world. ❧

couples' excursion to the Catskill Forest Preserve in New York, I was given the mission of finding some primo romantic turf. After hours of Internet searching I came up with nothing but conflicting reviews, so I finally made a frustrated call to the ranger station. The young, friendly female ranger immediately understood the pressure of planning a trip. She got my whole "we want to see some sexy nature stuff, but we're not all serious hikers" spiel. She said she knew the perfect spot. And she meant it. Once we made sense of the "round this tree, up that slope" directions, we were treated to a roomy site, perfect for our two love shacks, along a stream with great fishing, swimming, and sunbathing.

I haven't always been that lucky. I once called a ranger station five times, using different names and voices, to get past this particular woman who was hell-bent on giving me advice although she confessed that she had never actually hiked through the forest. Checking with the ranger station may not always tell you where to find the prettiest flowers in the park, but it's a necessary part of your planning.

Pirate's booty or fool's gold? All the homework I did to make sure the GLOK trip would be A+ for the virgin campers earned me a mediocre grade. Sure, the Kentucky weather was perfect, but the beautiful rock bridge we camped near turned out to be a crowded day hike destination. The information trail can be like a lucky treasure map smoothly leading right to the jewels, but sometimes the pirate turns out to be a one-eyed villain, and the X is just a decoy. 🐾

Two Trails Diverged in a Wood, I Chose the One Marked Easy

You've nailed down your forest or park. You know the section you're interested in, and you even know where to park the car. Should you follow the Loyalsock Trail, Sugar Run, or Bison Way? Consider your pack weight, physical strength, interests, group size, weather, terrain—a lot matters when picking the road to your new temporary home. How hard do you want to work? What do you really want to see? And how much do you want to bring? Two miles in to a site is a respectable but manageable distance for newbies, whereas a twelve-mile hike can be a three-day affair. Maybe you can do fifteen miles on city streets in heels and not even break a sweat, but four miles with a pack on is approaching the recommended limit for a novice. Some trails are loops with a central destination or a few popular stopping points; others are throughways and part of a larger network. Generally, loops offer fewer options for switching gears if the planned spot stinks; longer trails afford the possibility of continuing on or branching off if the mood strikes. Steep, wet, rocky—the trail conditions are as important as distance when choosing your route. That's where a guidebook with detailed descriptions comes in handy. Look for signs or *blazes*—color swatches on trees and rocks—to stick to your chosen path. And remember, itineraries are more flexible in the backcountry, so keep moving, double back, or stop early if you're ready to surrender.

Polka Dots or Plaid?

There are no stringent rules. Most likely, no decision is going to make or break your trip. Camping is the unvacation vacation—there's no steadfast schedule and there are always surprises. Experiment. Try something new with each outing. Develop your own system and style. You have complete creative license. Treat my suggestions like a paper doll set. Take what you like and leave what you don't. Dress your trip up in knee-highs and Mary Janes or a slinky gown and combat boots. Here are a few more trip-tailoring pointers I've picked up, mostly from fumbling all over the place.

Always Leave 'Em Wanting More

A pet iguana's needs might beckon you back from your camping trip, but your budget probably won't. Since cost is little

Don't get tripped up on terminology. Most of my excursions are called *base-camp trips*, meaning I hike to one spot, set up camp, and venture off from there on day jaunts. *Backpacking* traditionally refers to moving trips, a journey with a pack—hiking for distance and spending only one or two nights in each campsite. I usually hike *out and back* from the car along the same trail or take a short *loop* back to the parking lot. *Through-hiking* is walking and camping your way along a longer trail, starting the trip at one point and stopping at another. And where a trail originates, often intersecting with a road or parking lot, is the *trailhead*. 🐾

or no concern, you'll have to decide how long your trip will be based on other criteria. For a new camper, two nights is a fair amount of time in the wilderness. Day one gets eaten up with travel and setup, so a three-day trip allows one full day for wandering at will. There'll be some time to chill on day three, but don't forget the chores of breaking down the site, cleaning up, and hiking out. In the fragile days of your birth as a camper you don't want to miss home too much. Even a three-night excursion might leave you wanting more, but any more than that could send you packing. Once you fall in love with the adventure, three nights won't be enough. Since I've become a backcountry addict I rarely head out for less than four nights unless I only have time for a quickie. No matter how long your trip, try to pad the end of your vacation time with an extra day back home in the big city to pamper, recoup, and reintegrate.

High fives, not hair pulls. We leisurely hiked an easy one and three-quarter miles downhill to the GLOK campsite and kind of missed out on the chance to strut our victory dances. But on the uphill hike back out, hissing and scratching broke out over whose pack was the heaviest. The best hikes make you work just hard enough to feel badass but not hard enough to make you want to hurt your friends. Keep in mind that with a full pack on you'll be cruising along at about two miles per hour. Don't push yourself too much, but don't underestimate the bravado of making it. Fine-tune your happy hiking medium. ❧

Avoid Making Enemies

Every clock in my life is fast. My car: twenty-five minutes. Coffee machine: eighteen minutes. Alarm clock: a whopping fifty-five. These are my utterly ineffective attempts to be on time. Though I know the sun and the rangers wait for no one, I still arrive too late to camp.

To kick off our trip to Monongahela National Forest in West Virginia we diddled away time looking at truck-stop souvenirs and loitered in a fast-food joint. After leaving three hours later than planned, we shouldn't have been surprised when we pulled into the parking lot as dusk turned to night. Disoriented and freaked, we followed our flashlights into the blackness for our three-mile hike anyway. Every monstrous shadow and countless rustlings made us jump and squeal. When we finally made it to the waterfall we sought, we were wiped. Sleepy and sloppy, we set up camp for the night and woke to the sound of complaining campers just after sunrise. In daylight we were able to see we had set up camp in the middle of a trail, forcing plenty of peeved hikers to detour around our tent.

Trail trivia. There are eight National Scenic Trails spanning states, forests, parks, and wilderness lands. On the East Coast, the Appalachian Trail traces more than two thousand miles, from Maine to Georgia. And on the West Coast, her sister, the Pacific Crest Trail, runs almost three thousand miles from Mexico to Canada. It may not be your life's ambition to walk all those miles, but portions of these monumental trails make for great weekend excursions. 🐾

I've lost out on great sites, scraped my knees, and had to cancel whole trips just because of a late start. Even if you arrive just a little late, you might miss out on valuable wood-gathering time. Allow enough time to get lost on unfamiliar roads, hike at a comfortable pace, and still set up camp in daylight.

Be Wary of Meteorologists with Shiny Hair and Shinier Suits

Would you want to brush your teeth with cold water, huddled on a snow-covered balcony, while wearing gloves? Me neither. Once I grow bored with the challenges of warm-weather camping, I'll go completely insane and venture out in December. Until then I don't have much to offer in the way of advice for cold-weather camping other than: stay warm. Winter, even fall and early spring, can pose unique difficulties and require specialized gear. The capricious weather is enough to contend with in milder seasons. Seek the advice of the Weather Channel, the Farmer's Almanac, and a groundhog, then be prepared and go with the flow. If there's a slight chance of rain, throw in a poncho. (A light jacket is a handy addition no matter what the weather brings—use it to kneel on, make a welcome mat, or throw a

There was an unusual quiet during the planning stages of the GLOK trip until Rachel burst out with, "Does anyone else care about freezing their ass off?" Once we properly commiserated, the silent suffering lifted. Prepared for a chilly November trip, we were pleased with Kentucky's high temperatures. But despite our windfall, the outcry was unanimous: "What's camping without tank tops?" ❧

picnic.) If it's been unusually cool, bring thermal knits and a hat. Reconsider the trip if something more severe is predicted, but don't be surprised if the calamity never arrives.

Beyond Grass and Trees

On Fire Island we endured painful sand fleabites almost any time we stood still in daylight. On the Florida coast, my legs sweated so much, they developed an aggravating rash. And

---

Reply hazy, try again. Read the sky, study the smoke, and listen to the wind. Grade-school science classes evaded me, but science is actually cool when it applies. Baffle your troops by busting out with weather predictions.

- Can't tell a nimbostratus from a cumulonimbus? That's okay. Watch out for rain when clouds are low, gray, and ominous, or tall and layered like a huge wedding cake. Rest easy when clear skies are dotted with thick, white, cotton-ball clouds.

- If your campfire smoke rises up evenly, the weather should stay clear. If it seems to come back down and linger in camp, a storm may be in your future.

- Red sky at night, nature girl's delight. Red sky in the morning, nature girl's warning.

- You know the saying about a quiet before the storm? You know how in that quiet every sound seems magnified? When you can hear things from afar very clearly, a storm is usually in the cards. 🐾

A few ordinary tips for extraordinary trips

- Take it easy. Fatigue comes quickly in any harsh environment. Relax during the sun's peak hours.

- Drink a lot. Campers need two to three quarts of water per day, but in the severe sun you'll need more. Also, water sources may be scarce; bring all you'll need with you if necessary.

- Cover up. Hot as it may be, wear long sleeves and pants to protect yourself from exposure. Sunscreen, sunglasses, and a wide-brimmed hat are musts.

- Deserts are prone to flash floods. A campsite in a bank, ravine, or dry riverbed could float away.

- Pack cozy pajamas. Days may be hot, but nights can get cold in the desert and at the beach.

- Gear up. Longer tent stakes are helpful in sand, and thick-soled shoes are a necessity in the desert. Don't skimp on supplies that might make for smoother sailing.

- Speaking of sailing, stick to calm waters. You don't need much experience for a canoe or kayak trip on a gentle river, but don't brave whitewater without a skilled paddler. An added bonus of boating: your vessel can lug lots more supplies than your back.

- Go off-season. Take these trips in spring or fall, not when the sun is strongest. ❖

after my first canoe camping trip, down the Delaware, I nursed my swollen sun-poisoned face for a week. A common vision of camping is lush green and warm brown, but ruddy deserts and pastel beaches also beckon wanderers with tents. And blue waters call to canoeists and kayakers. These are seriously special but strenuous trips. The endless sand and enveloping water are thrilling, drastic changes from our paved and seeded surroundings. Waves lull you into a deep sleep. The sky never seems bluer and hair never looks better than when it's blown by sea air. You'll return strong and revived. But unless you take precautions, there can be heavy penalties for such a mythic experience. Know what you're up against and be as prepared as possible. In the desert, drinking water is scarce and the sun brutal. Sandy beaches are ten times harder to traverse with a pack, and often there's not a speck of shade. Floating down a river, the sun beats down from above and reflects up from below. These exceptional journeys are worth every challenge; just do the research, heed the precautions (see sidebar), and invest in special gear to make sure your trip is a success.

Exterior Design

Legs ready to declare mutiny? Slip out of that pack and seek out your site. Stick to preexisting campsites to keep wear and tear to a minimum. A small sign, a clear rock ring, or a flat clearing with logs arranged for sitting are sure indications. If you must start a camp from scratch, set up two hundred

Scribble this. Take a page out of my journal—a site sketch from the Finger Lakes (my first site ever) to help you craft a campsite even Martha Stewart might approve.

- Go the distance. Secure food and trash one hundred feet from the tent. It's safest to cook one hundred feet downwind of your tent, too, so bears don't mistake you for a walking biscuit. (FYI: one hundred feet equals about forty steps.)

- Do your dirty work (poop, pee, and wash up) two hundred feet from camp, trails, and water sources.

- Don't be a sucker for clear skies. Hang your tarp, even if it's sunny, for a ready hideout in case it rains. Stash firewood and other goodies under there for protection.

- Set up a water bucket or basin away from camp to store and do dirty dishes. Disperse gray water over a big area, two hundred feet from camp, trails, and water sources.

- Let it flow. Hang a water jug or bag from a branch to create a flowing faucet.

- Scatter dishrags around camp so there's always somewhere to wipe dirty hands other than pants or valuable paper products.

- Be invisible. When you break camp, pick up every last bit of plastic and untie every string—it should look like no one was ever there. 🐾

feet from trails, water sources, and cliffs. Follow any special rules—stay off dunes and away from protected wildlife areas. Scout out a site that's somewhat flat, level, and mostly clear of plants. Try to find dry, high ground, which will mean fewer bugs and less-damp butts. Sites are as varied as the campers who choose them. In Virginia, I clamored for a hidden nook nestled behind two dunes, whereas a big group set up a central camp in the middle of everything, and a couple scouted out a tiny peak for their compact tent. A mixture of shade and sun is preferable, and proximity to water is not only practical, it's wonderful. There's no hurry; take off your pack and stroll around. The perfect site often pops up.

Creating a welcoming, efficient, comfy site satisfies do-it-yourself cravings. Work out your rearranging and redecorating urges with a clean slate in the great wide open. Start with a level spot for the tent. Clear away rocks and sticks. Fluff up dry leaves or sand for extra padding. Now pitch the tent, but before you stake it to the ground, place it on the area you're considering. Crawl in and go for a test drive. Level? Soft? Is your head higher that your feet? If not, you'll wake to a headache. Keep trying. Go sideways or try diagonal. This can take a while. Have someone else try it out too. Shift your head and the tent until you home in on the exact spot, then seal the deal by staking it down.

Once the tents are pitch perfect, get the living room ready for maximum cozy. Where fires are allowed, the campfire is usually camp's main hangout. Check the fire ring. Is there a stable, even wall of rocks in place? If not, rebuild it. Rocks keep the fire from spreading and make a decent ottoman for warming tired feet (as long as you're careful). Designate a team of gatherers to collect dry wood, and create a wood pile a safe distance from the fire. Most likely your site has been used before and there are log couches and rock recliners around the fire. If not, invent your own. Use flat low rocks as tables for cooking, cutting, and cards. Roll instead of lifting heavy stuff. But be cautious and disrupt as little as possible—those logs and rocks are home to many critters.

Next, design the bathroom and stock the pantry. "Bathroom" is used creatively here. It's really more like a branch where toiletries, toilet paper, and a towel are hung. Trees or rocks serve as great markers for organized supplies. You'll have the bathroom stump, the kitchen rock, and the garbage bag tree. Separating areas according to needs is like creating a blueprint for a house. It's the best way to keep track of things. When you go for a pee run in the middle of the night, you'll know exactly where to reach for the wipes. Keep all your ziplock bags in one spot, and you'll always know how many you have left. String

The GLOK's hearts sank when we made it to our planned destination and found three disappointing, muddy campsites. But we split up and scoured the place. Turned out the three wet spots surrounded a hill, at the top of which was a perfectly dry, covert site. Not only were we muck-free all weekend, but from higher ground we could see other hikers but they couldn't see us. 🐾

Protect that Gruyère from greedy paws. In most forests and parks, food and trash should be hung safely out of the reach of bears, raccoons, boar, mice, and other scavengers with a taste for people treats. I use an old messenger bag as my hanging camp cupboard, but any sturdy, preferably waterproof, bag will do. Anything scented, even toothpaste, must be hung. And double bagging trash before you hoist it is a good idea too. Never store food or trash in or near your tent. Not only does the scent attract the beastly snouts, bugs will also come knocking.

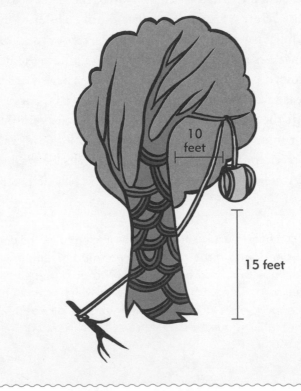

10 feet

15 feet

There's an easy way to get food and trash hung even if you're five foot three and on the wimpy side (like me). The GLOK, fat and lethargic from a gooey dinner of cheesy polenta, all groaned in unison when it was time to hang the bear bag. Laura stepped up to the plate, and the rest of us cheered and clapped behind her. Getting it up there can sometimes feel like a reality game-show challenge. Find a tree with a thick limb about twenty feet up. Tie one end of a piece of long rope (fifty feet or so) to the bag, and the other end to a hefty arm-length stick. Toss the stick over the middle of the branch. Make sure the rope rests about ten feet away from the tree's trunk. Now pull on the stick. Start walking away from the tree with stick in hand. Voila—the bag rises. Keep walking until the bag is about fifteen feet off the ground. Once it's high enough, wrap the stick and slack rope around the trunk of a nearby tree.

Food-hanging can be difficult when there's not a suitable tree in sight. On the beach, for example, food must sometimes be buried due to a lack of tall trees. And camping in serious bear country requires more severe precautions: many parks and forests are beginning to require bear canisters, which are bear-proof containers made for food, trash, and even sunscreen—anything that might smell good to a bear. Bears have wised up. They know our little tricks, and they like our mini pizzas. Unfortunately, as bears have grown accustomed to campers, they've become more bold and aggressive. For obvious reasons this is bad for us, but it's also bad for the bears—a bear that makes a move for people food may have to be killed.

continued on page 48

continued from page 47

Bear canisters cost about seventy bucks, weigh around three pounds, and look kind of like cylindrical breadboxes. Since everyone eats different stuff in different quantities, the amount of food the canisters hold is debatable. Canisters require diligent menu planning and occasional sacrifice— canned goods, fruit, and bread will probably take up too much valuable space. But they certainly take the worry out of finding good trees and the hassle out of getting your stash up there. Just lock the canister up and leave it about a hundred feet from camp. Those paws can scratch all they want; they won't be able to get at the chewy center.

Research the land you're visiting and check with a ranger for special precautions before you head out. Not only do places like Yosemite National Park, Sierra National Forest, Olympic National Park, Adirondack State Park, and just about any-where in Alaska require canisters, they also ask that you use only approved makes and models. Some sites make it easy on campers by offering canisters for rent. My usual mantra: do your homework and be prepared. Better safe than faced with defending a can of kidney beans from killer claws. ❧

up a clothesline, and you'll not only remember where you put your wet towel, you'll have a curtain to change behind. Folks are less likely to leave trash lying around when they know the bag is a few paces away. Avoid chaos and constant cleaning. Get organized from the start.

🐾 🐾 🐾 🐾 🐾

Visualize your favorite T-shirt hanging from this clothesline. Imagine sharing ghost stories with your best buddies lined up on these logs and warmed by your very own campfire. Picture crawling out of your tent in the morning to a vista of green and the fresh smell of soil. Are you itching for your own primitive palace yet? Onward to chapter 3. Time to gear up for your maiden voyage.

Squirreling Away the Nuts (and Bolts)

The gear essentials, where to get them, and how to use them.

My first camping experience was a wild afterthought, a sudden spontaneous adventure, so I've been accustomed to makeshift camping gear from the start. I brought a comforter as a sleeping bag; a $75 tent (laughable in the camping kingdom); a borrowed backpack; and for water, a forty-pound, five-gallon jug. I've since bought a toasty yet light sleeping bag filled with magical insulating materials and a pricey but essential water purifier, also enchanted by the convenient-camping elves. But my original cheapo tent with the cigarette hole I burned in it on that first time out is still my trusty home-in-a-bag, and making a round of last-minute calls to finagle a backpack out of a camping comrade has become a pretrip ritual. It might seem senseless to camp as much as I do yet be reluctant to invest in the best gear. I'll try to explain. (Warning: camping heresy on the way.) For some, the lure of camping is the sport—so, reasonably, to conquer and compete, specialty gear engineered for speed and productivity is in order. To be fair, I don't think Gore-Tex types are necessarily as focused on winning as they are intent on pushing their limits and testing their bodies. I prefer to keep my camping more of an easygoing endeavor. Out there I get to pretend I'm instinctual and uncontrived, and for once, that means improvise, not buy. Camping is my weekend pilgrimage to a more centered, natural self. Expensive, processed, complicated, synthetic stuff emblazoned with reflective logos and sold at megastores is not only unnecessary, it just doesn't jibe with my lay-low philosophy. Plus, my finances are already spread thin between a passion for concocting exotic dishes with hard-to-find ingredients and an

Gadget girl? Got some money to burn? State of the art turns you on? Here's my most-wanted list of backcountry luxuries.

- **Sleeping Pad**—I've made it this far without ever touching one, but I'd be remiss if I didn't admit that most campers swear by them. Closed-cell, open-cell, self-inflating— slipped under your sleeping bag, they all provide a lightweight yet inviting cushion. Depending on how much you're plagued by the pea, spend $10 or $100.

  Thrifty Girl's Substitute: Lay your sleeping bag down over a few layers of clothes or pitch your tent on a bed of dry, fluffy leaves.

- **Headlamp**—Not only is playing Uno in the dark with a flashlight in your mouth difficult, it hurts your teeth. A headlamp is just that—a small light that straps onto your forehead, illuminating wherever you look. Think obsession with vintage earrings and purses, not to mention rent, utilities, loans, and good wine.

So what do I get for all this piety? Usually an achy butt because I don't own a sleeping pad, an item on every camper's list. But my backwoods approach has also helped me get out more, reach a tranquility unheard-of for most hotheaded neurotic types, and save more fun funds for Trader Joe's and yard sales. A lack of expensive, newfangled gear doesn't have to keep us from occasionally lounging under the stars and catching a few breaths of fresh air.

Even if you plan to eventually outfit your trips with the latest equipment, I recommend you borrow, rent, or buy used

---

spelunkers—they're pretty cool. Also, pretty pricey. A good headlamp can cost $60.

Thrifty Girl's Substitute: Invest in a thin finger-sized flashlight; they're easier to hold in your hand and between your teeth.

- **Carabiner Cup**—Traditionally, a carabiner is a metal ring with a latch used for climbing; novelty carabiners come in pretty colors and attach things, like cups or keys, to packs. These Carabiner Cups are $10 creations whose handles are already carabiners. Talk about novelty.

Thrifty Girl's Substitute: $1 carabiner + $4 cup

- **Camp Espresso Maker**—It weighs less than a pound and can serve up two dark, hearty shots at a time. It's also stainless steel, cute, and about $30.

Thrifty Girl's Substitute: Thrifty Girl is speechless. ❧

gear first. Gear is both expensive and quirky. You don't want to discover you prefer a top-loading backpack or a down sleeping bag after you've thrown down the big bucks for other types. Start out by borrowing as much as you can—old camping gear is commonly tucked away in attics and garages after just a few uses. Check thrift stores, eBay, and classifieds (think Craigslist and your local paper, too)—you'd be surprised by the quality of gear you can score secondhand. Lots of people indulged in the seventies' campout nature thing only to surrender to Disneyland. Skulk around the camping forums—there are lots of eager gear swappers and resellers. Call local camping stores—some are nice enough to offer rentals, a great way to test out the goods. If you have no luck with these backdoor methods, there are always the superstores—REI, Campmor, Coleman, and Eastern Mountain Sports. They carry everything you need to pull a Jane Goodall, and they frequently have sales. One of my favorite online retailers, Backcountry, tests everything they sell and runs a wacky one-item-per-day über-sale that feels like shopping and gambling all at once. (Links, links, and more links, including one to Backcountry, are all waiting for you in the resources section of this book.) The nationwide monster chains—the kind hawking everything from groceries to clothes—also sell inexpensive gear. It's not top-notch, but it will do the trick.

Wherever you decide to spend your money, read the reviews first. There's not one piece of gear, manufacturer, or model that has not been reviewed by a camping magazine or campers in forums. That said, gear is constantly evolving; it's hard to keep up. In the quest for camping gear you're constantly juggling price, weight, efficiency, comfort, and the harder-to-quantify personal preference. Luckily, you don't need much to get started. Here's a rundown of the five big-ticket items you'll want to gather up for your first nature-girl experience.

Tent

I was schooled on the spectrum of tents when I went on my first group trip to Assateague Island. A frugal fellow with a tent even cheaper than mine lost his rain fly (a tent-tailored tarp) thanks to severe wind and faulty secures. A horny couple sweated the weekend away in an egg-shaped—and sized—dome that, although quite fancy, could never suit claustrophobic folk. A group of three pitched a tent that looked like a cabin with poles the size of my forearms. My mid-size, acceptable for four but best for two, charming (yet inexpensive) tent was the local hotspot. Roomy enough for Yahtzee but sufficiently cozy for a shared hot toddy, it was where everyone clamored to be after the chill of dark took over.

Tents are labeled by both the seasons and the number of people they comfortably accommodate. Any three-season tent will be perfect in warmer weather. Keep in mind, bigger and cheaper almost always means heavier in any camping gear. And as with all things camping, weight is paramount in selecting a tent. Don't skimp entirely on homeyness just to shave off a pound or two, especially if you've got a partner to split the load. Most two or three-person tents weigh between four and nine pounds. My tent comes in just over nine, but when the time comes to retire the old gal, I'll aim for a more modest seven.

Weight isn't the only concern when tent shopping—a good tent is also weatherproof and well-ventilated. First, a quick anatomy lesson. Tents generally include three components: (1) the body or the main cabin; (2) the *rain fly*, a piece of waterproof fabric that protects the tent like a raincoat; and (3) the poles and stakes. The cabin should be made of light, water-resistant fabric, and the seams should be double-stitched, covered, or taped to prevent leaking. Look for a cabin floor with a built-in water-

Tent tips to treasure

- A-frame, dome, cabin, hexagon—tents come in interesting shapes. Pick your favorite form.

- Mesh skylights are coveted—gaze at the stars without insect visitors, and glimpse the sunrise from the warm cocoon of your sleeping bag.

- Freestanding and single-walled are newer tent trends, but word has it they're not worth the extra money. Freestanding tents still need to be staked down or they can blow away. And to the makers of single-walled (meaning the rain fly is one with the main cabin) tents I say, if it ain't broke, don't fix it.

- If your tent must be pitched over a separate ground cover, don't let any of it peek out the sides, or it will become a basin for water. Take a walk around the tent and tuck in any visible edges.

- Seam sealer is sold in every camping store for just a few bucks. Brush it onto leaky or worn seams to keep your abode dry.

proof bottom. Mine has a *bathtub floor*, like a tarp that comes up a few inches on all sides. If a waterproof floor isn't included, spend the extra money on a ground cover (or make your own using a tarp or any heavy duty plastic) to pitch your tent on, or you'll have a soggy slumber. Insist on ample mesh windows for a bright, airy feel. My tent also has a *vestibule*, which I lovingly call "the porch." A vestibule is a covered area outside the tent door for storing dirty shoes and poking heads into early

- Pitch your tent a few times before the big day, but don't be embarrassed to bring along the assembly directions or a cheat sheet.

- For easier carrying, divvy the tent parts among your tent mates. Tie the poles onto one pack; stuff the stakes and rain fly into another, and the cabin into a third.

- Do a quick inventory of parts before you head out and when you break down camp. Campsites are the Lands of Lost Stakes.

- Tents inevitably get littered with bits of outdoor funk. Pull the stakes, turn the tent on its side, and shake the grime out through the front door. Imagine if house cleaning were that easy?

- Back at home, be sure to pitch your tent once more to air it out before packing it away till next time. And if your nose suspects mildew in every nook and cranny (like mine does), religiously air out your tent before trips too. 🐾

morning air. A rain fly is pretty standard on most tents; make sure one is included. Poles are usually either aluminum or fiberglass. Aluminum is lauded for its durability, although I've never had a problem with my fiberglass poles. Jenga can confuse me in the wrong light, but I've never encountered an unpitchable tent. Just make sure yours doesn't require a complicated method that could render you homeless if it's dark or raining when you arrive. Other perks to shop for: extra stakes, pockets for stashing lip balm or tissues, a *gear loft* up above for turning a flashlight into a chandelier, and a stuff sack to store it all. Check the online reviews, chew the ears off salespeople, and go for a test drive. If you're forking over $100 to $500, make sure you're happy with your new mobile pad.

Inseparable and (a little) indolent. Rather than use two separate tents for our GLOK outing, we opted for the camaraderie of a huge six-person tent borrowed from Laura's man. We gracefully shared the responsibility of carrying the twenty-pound behemoth, but its life was repeatedly threatened. With a straight face, Rachel rationalized that leaving it pitched somewhere with a "Free Tent" sign would be a generous gesture. There was a semiserious discussion about chipping in to buy Todd a new one for Christmas. But in the end it was worth bringing on the trip and lugging home. The tent was heftier and bigger than we needed, but it was an awesome no-boys-allowed clubhouse and even accommodated an impromptu dance party. A big tent is not sustainable if camping becomes a regular hobby, but, like wearing stilettos, it can be worth the occasional suffering. 🐾

Sleeping Bag

About fifteen outings went by before I got a verifiable sleeping bag. Camp life prebag was authentically hobo but nowhere near as cozy. I would tightly roll up a full-sized blanket, tie it to my backpack, and sandwich myself in it for sleeping. The blanket roll worked fine, although it was occasionally cumbersome on the trail and sometimes chilly at night. It can also flop about and sometimes unfurl if not tied evenly or tight enough to a backpack. The blanket roll is perfect for beginners who can't find someone willing to lend a sleeping bag, but down the line a good sleeping bag is a worthwhile investment. The first night I spent in my first sleeping bag was nothing short of wondrous.

The two things to look for in a sleeping bag are warmth and light weight. Most material is not both toasty and lightweight at the same time, so sleeping bags are scientifically engineered and, therefore, not cheap. Think somewhere between $75 and $300. The filling, either down or synthetic, is the heart of a bag. Generally, down is light but super warm. It's also expensive, prone to clumping (leaving cold spots), and if wet, utterly

Get inspired. One of the highlights of visiting camping stores is the painfully cute miniature gear on display—teensy tents and wee sleeping bags. Even if you don't plan on buying, check out the absurd adorable replicas—like the Barbie dream house, minus the overwhelming pink. Bring a miniature version of yourself, and you can pretend you're roughing it in gorgeous Big Sur. Just make sure no one's watching. 🐾

useless and smelly. Synthetics are heavier but more resilient. They're also constantly upgraded and streamlined, so most synthetic fill materials made today are simply dreamy. There's PrimaLoft, Thermolite, Polarguard—the list goes on and on. Read the reviews first. Does the bag stay fluffy? Does the fill stay in place? Is it as warm as promised?

Sleeping bags are given temperature ratings. If a bag says thirty degrees, then supposedly you'll be a happy camper as long as it doesn't drop below thirty. But how many times have you suffered, shivering in a car with the air conditioner pumping, while the driver was obliviously content? Temperature ratings are not specific to your body, and worse, they're exaggerated. Fortunately, that doesn't matter much to warm-weather campers. A bag rated to about twenty degrees should never fail you in moderate weather. Seek warmth, but don't be weighed down by your bag. Five pounds is a lot for a sleeping bag; a three-pound bag is ideal.

Sleeping bags come in mummy, rectangle, and sometimes a modified mummy variety. Mummy bags are tapered, smaller, snugger, and therefore lighter and warmer, but rectangle bags offer more room for tossing and turning. It's really up to you. Mine is a slight mummy—it tapers at the bottom but not as much as some. It also doesn't have a hood, included on many mummy models. Women's versions are also available to fit smaller frames. If you have a willing camping partner, look for mated bags that can be zipped together for private pajama parties. Check for a draft tube—a strip of fabric that stops air from sneaking in through the zipper—and a small stuff sack for easy compressing and packing. Stuffing, instead of rolling, a sleeping bag helps keep it fluffy, and it's a hell of a lot easier to do. In case of rain, pop the stuff sack into a garbage bag before you head out on the trail. Back at home, store your sleeping bag in a pillowcase so it can breathe.

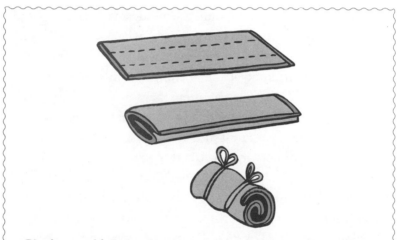

Blanket sushi. Before I was spoiled by my sleeping bag, I blissfully passed camp nights in a blanket. The old-school blanket roll is easy and absolutely adequate for beginners. Lay a full or queen-sized blanket out on the floor and fold the width in thirds. Then, kneeling over one end, slowly and tightly roll until it resembles sushi. Take two three-foot lengths of rope and tie up both sides of your roll. Now it can be tied to the top or bottom of a backpack. Center it so it doesn't pull you one way or the other as you hike. Use a fleece blanket if you've got one—fleece is lightweight but warm. Double your pleasure by sewing together two blankets along the bottom and one side. Then roll it up the same way. 🐾

Backpack

A comfortable backpack makes tough hikes bearable, and an uncomfortable backpack could make any camper hate camping. Since I always borrow, I've become acquainted with all sorts of pack woes—faulty zippers, straps that dig trenches in skin, and poor fits that bounce around, smacking your head with every step. This is one bit of gear where a women's version is key. Female bags are tailored for torso lengths (between your hips and the knob at the bottom of your neck) of twelve to seventeen inches, whereas men's bags are suited for a tall sixteen to twenty-two. Longer bags don't rest properly on our hips, making for crankiness and cursing.

The second most important thing to look for in a backpack is its carrying capacity, measured in cubic inches. Anywhere around 3,000 or 4,000 cubic inches is ideal for weekend trips. Check for lumbar padding to protect your back, and sturdy, cushioned straps and hip belt. Packs are framed with internal or

There will be prancing sheep, egrets, snails, chipmunks—if you're lucky, maybe meerkats—to help you count your way to siesta, but unless you're determined to bear the extra bulk, there won't be a fluffy pillow. You could spend anywhere between $5 and $20 on a camping pillow, but you'd do just as well making your own. Inflate a big ziplock bag and dress it up in a soft T-shirt. Use your sleeping bag's stuff sack, or bring a pillowcase, and fill it with clothes. Truth is, camping tuckers you out so thoroughly, a folded newspaper would work. ❧

external supports. Internal frames, or stays, offer more support, flexibility, and a closer fit. External frame bags tend to feel like a tin can on your back. Try them on and compare. A backpack should fit like a glove—make sure the straps adjust perfectly to your body. My heart skips a beat when I see lots of zippered pockets to keep me organized and loops for tying on my cup, cooking pot, or sleeping bag. As for how a bag should load— top, side, front—that's up to you. I've found top-loading bags are a pain when I want my flip-flops and they're all the way at the bottom. A decent pack can be found for around $100, but a deluxe pack can run up to $400.

Water Purifier

When I started camping I didn't even consider what a hot commodity water would be, especially since, like most civilized girls, I expect clean running water at the twist of a knob. From brewing morning coffee to making lentil burgers to washing muddy hands, water is essential to backcountry pleasures. Not to mention, camping is thirsty work and water is heavy. Luckily there are tried-and-true solutions to getting potable water in the wild, but none are perfect. Contrast and compare until the cows come home (as I have); there are minor drawbacks to all the methods. Until there are fresh-water faucets in the wilderness, we have to settle on whichever system strikes us as most tolerable. As you probably guessed, sooner or later some sacrifice is required to get primitive. Getting clean water is probably the biggest backcountry hassle, but it's still not as bad as helping your best friend move into the third story of a walk-up in August. Here's how I learned to stop carrying absurd water weight and love my portable purifier.

Back when I was still picking my nose in public, people were camping. These early campers drank freely from any clear water they stumbled on in the backcountry. That innocent era is over. It is no longer safe to drink out of rivers, streams, lakes, or ponds. Can you even fathom a time when it was? Bacteria, protozoa, cysts, and even viruses can be lurking in any wild water source (not to mention in wells and reservoirs) and can cause anything from weeklong diarrhea to hepatitis. My original solution for these microscopic cooties was to fill a five-gallon jug from the tap in my tub. Five gallons can roughly cover two people's drink-

Bottoms up. A widely accepted rule is that in moderate weather, campers need two to three quarts of water a day just for drinking. Always bring some from home in case you can't find a decent source to purify. Canteens, which sling over your shoulder, distribute weight away from your already burdened back. They're also great for quick sips on the trail. Dehydration is serious stuff when you're exerting and sweating. At first you may be very thirsty and your pee, extra yellow. These are early signs—pay attention to them. Drink up slowly. Take it easy. And if you're not a big water drinker, consider toting a few sports drinks for quick hydration. It's okay to fess up—yes, water is life's liquid, it's three-quarters of the earth's surface, it's the favored drink of supermodels, yet some of us just don't like it. Sports drinks come in the powdered variety now, so carrying is easy. If anybody asks, just say Parker Posey swears by them. ❧

ing, cooking, and washing needs for a three-day trip. But a five-gallon jug weighs more than my backpack weighs full. Carrying that damn thing forty feet requires six breaks; any more than that requires kicking, screaming, and crying. It's ludicrous to rely on this method. Now I fill a quart-sized canteen in the kitchen sink, sneak a few pint-sized water bottles into my pack, boil water for cooking, and once what I've brought runs out, filter water through my handy purifier for drinking.

All the creeps in water can be killed by simply boiling for about five minutes. The only problem with boiling water is that it's time consuming and it produces hot water—not very refreshing. But it works, it's easy, and it's cheap. Boil a big supply ahead of time on a camp stove and store it in a folding basin or jug. This will give it time to cool. If you go this route, make sure you have plenty of stove fuel. (What fuel? What stove? The one you'll need to feed your hungry troop. Hang in there; chapter 5 sorts out all things yummy.) Some people find boiling inconvenient, so they opt for a purifier or a filter. Purifiers remove about 99.9 percent of the nastiness; filters claim to get everything but viruses. Both are pretty pricey. If you do invest in one, go all the way and get a purifier. There are tons of articles on water purification. Some retailers offer explanations on their websites to help people understand the scientific stuff before they buy. Not only is it complicated, the technology is constantly changing. Most important feature to look for: an absolute pore size of 0.2 micron. The smaller the pore size, the fewer harmful things can pass through. Read up on the elements used to purify. Iodine is a popular addition for

The Wilderness Clutch: A Daypack

Much like a clutch purse for a night out on the town, you'll need something small to carry just the important items—map, sandwich, water bottle, lip gloss, camera—for afternoon expeditions from camp. Some backpacks include removable small knapsacks or fanny packs. Fanny packs are traditional hiker attire. I gave my mom hell for wearing one in the nineties; there's no way I could convince myself to strap one on now. A student's backpack makes a fine daypack, but you could also get crafty. Recycle an old pair of jeans and create a simple drawstring carryall with personality.

GATHER UP

Sewing machine
Old pair of jeans with belt loops
Sewing needle and thread
Stick pins
One 3- to 4-foot length of
   cord and two matching or
   coordinating 3- to 6-inch pieces

Front

1. Lay the jeans face up on a flat surface. Zipper and button them shut. If the fly won't stay securely fastened, hand stitch it closed.

2. Fold each leg at the knee, toward the waistband. Center the bottom of each leg between the first and second belt loop, on either side of the zipper. You may have to fold in the sides, especially if you're

Back

working with boot-leg jeans. Once you've folded the leg width to fit in the space between the belt loops, fold over the ends of the legs one inch toward the waistband. Line up the folded legs with the top of the waistband and pin them in place between the loops.

3. Sew two $1/4$-inch seams along the top of the waistband, between the belt loops, attaching each pant leg. Be careful not to stitch the belt loops shut.

4. Where the pant legs fold, tie the shorter pieces of cord decoratively.

5. Run the longer piece of cord through the belt loops, just like you would a belt, but with the two ends meeting at the rear instead of the fly. This is the top of your pack—the cord is the drawstring and the legs are your straps.

NOTES

- The butt of the jeans is actually the front of your pack, so the cuter the pockets, the better. Time to recycle those too-big Sergio Valentes.

- Add sticky-backed Velcro tabs or colored snaps to fasten the back pockets for safely carrying small stuff.

- Neckties, scarves, and colored cotton clothesline also make great drawstrings.

- The Scouts rig a version of this daypack right at camp. Use two pieces of cord to close the bottoms of the legs and tie them to the belt loops on either side of the zipper. Use the longer cord to make a drawstring through the loops, and you've got a temporary pack. When you return from your hike, untie the cords and slip the jeans back on.

killing viruses, but it can upset thyroid functioning. I like my purifier because it uses a chemical-free system. On the other hand, it can't be taken apart or cleaned on the trail. A filter that can be maintained in the field is a big plus, since these things clog frequently. With many purifiers and filters, a tiring rou-

Hydration hints

- Trail guides or maps will occasionally point to springs, one of the cleanest wild water sources, but rivers, streams, and lakes are also fair game. Watch out for small pools of still water—they're incubators for microorganisms.

- Bandanas and coffee filters work as prefilters to remove sediments, which means less clogging of your precious purifier.

- Folding jugs or collapsing basins are great for storing a big supply of purified water. Some jugs also have a little loop for easy hanging from a tree for a faux faucet.

- Filters and purifiers need regular cleaning and maintenance. Follow the manufacturer's directions—this is one piece of equipment you don't want to have fail.

- Pack lemon juice, herbal tea bags, or powdered drink mixes to flavor water that doesn't taste like your preferred bottled brand.

- One way to get around the water purifying process: if you're certain you'll be camping less than two miles from the car, pack some 2.5 gallon refrigerator boxes of water in the trunk. Designate a water crew to make a second trip while you set up camp. ❧

tine of pumping, cleaning, and clogging is par for the course. Like I said, nothing's perfect. Do your homework. Be prepared to spend anywhere between $50 and $200. And stick with reliable manufacturers, known for their years of proven experience in delivering safe water to campers: Katadyn, MSR, SweetWater, and First Need.

It's also good practice to have a back-up water plan. I carry a few chlorine dioxide tablets, available in camping stores, in case all else fails—my purifier clogs or I run out of stove fuel. These can be dropped into a liter of water and after a few hours the water is safe. They're cheap and good in emergencies. Beware of iodine tablets. They were popular in the past but are potentially harmful to our precious glands and taste terrible. An intriguing new system has also cropped up. I almost wish my purifier would break so I could justify spending another heap of money on water purification. The SteriPEN is a small sterilizing wand, weighing less than four ounces. It uses ultraviolet light rays and requires just a few stirrings to neutralize everything harmful. It sounds too good to be true—it can purify one quart of water in less than two minutes. The drawbacks: it's expensive and will eventually require a pricey replacement bulb. Still, this magic pen is currently my most coveted piece of camping gear. Until I bite the bullet, or a mad scientist devises a way to kill every evil thing in every drop of water, my triceps get a light workout pumping my purifier. None of these methods is as much of a no-brainer as turning the blue or red faucet handle, but that's why we bother with camping: it gives our brains a hiatus from typical worries and offers up new puzzles to solve. Primitive life is an invitation to live more consciously, right down to something as taken for granted as clean drinking water.

Tarp

In an attempt to patch up our floundering relationship, a boyfriend once recommended that we spend a romantic night in a campground. This would be considered my first foray into camping, except we were cramped in the hatchback of his car instead of in the hole-filled tent we borrowed. Turns out moths like tent fabric and rain doesn't stop for two people trying to rekindle their flames. We watched through steamy windows (thanks to the wet weather, not the wet hot love) as the couple at the next site grilled hot dogs and guzzled beer under the canopy they had created with their tarp.

A tarp is straightforward. It's a piece of sturdy waterproof material with grommets—reinforced holes—for easy hanging. Think shelter, shed, raincoat, and ground cover. Camping stores sell durable tarps for about $20; any more than that is robbery. My $14 tarp has lasted three years. Ten by ten feet will suffice in most situations. True, trash bags can do many things a tarp can, but since tarps are cheap and light, there's really no excuse for not owning one. A shower curtain is a better thrifty gal's substitute. And trash bags (as we know from the time we leaked raw chicken all over the linoleum and kitty wouldn't stop licking it up and then puked all night) tear easily. Tarps are also useful at home for protecting the floor from messy art projects, covering the barbecue grill, and throwing a rainproof party on the patio.

When you've mastered the building of a tarp lean-to, you may not be able to suppress a howl. No single synthetic item has ever made me feel so feral.

A Few More for the Road

That's it for the big camping hitters, but anything else—from flashlights to work gloves—that I wouldn't dream of bringing on a regular vacation is also included on my *Gear* list (see pages 189–90). You might find a lot of this stuff in your apartment, back home in your parent's shed, in a hardware store, or at a corner bodega. Some of these supplies may make your forehead crinkle or your eyes roll or maybe your heart race. I know I've said it before, but if I can do this, you can too. Think crafty. Improvise. Conjure up ancient primordial wisdom. Have fun—it doesn't have to be as intense as the pages of the hardcore outdoor magazines make it look. Braid rope into a hammock. Experiment with catching rainwater in a duct-tape bucket. Illuminate camp with lanterns made from aluminum foil. Live out your *Gilligan's Island* fantasies. Are you the Professor or Mary Ann? Here's a list of essentials any shipwrecked voyager would be thrilled to have, and some suggestions for using them.

Aluminum Foil
Every backcountry chef has an affinity for foil. (Don't fret—food, booze, and kitchen contraptions are covered in chapter 5.) Even if you're not a foodie, a few squares of aluminum foil are a backcountry necessity. Put a lid on boiling water, wrap up leftovers, form drinking cups, and shape swans for a swan race.

Fold up six 8 by 8-inch sheets and slide them into a book—
you're guaranteed to find a use for them.

Bug Repellent

Vile insects are my sworn enemies, and unfortunately they
usually win all our battles. Until I can calmly watch a cricket
hop across my shoe or take the "just stay still" approach to a
bee, I bring industrial-sized, extremely powerful, yet potentially harmful to unborn children, DEET bug spray. I'm sorry,
environment. I'm sorry, woodland animals. I'm even (kind of)
sorry, bugs. I just can't budge on this. For the brave, there are
safer, gentler, natural sprays and creams sold in camping and
health food stores.

Camping Shovel

Brace yourself, this could be the hardest one to swallow. You'll
need a small shovel to dig cat holes. As in, you'll need it to make
the holes you will grow to accept as your backcountry toilets.
No, really. (Don't worry. I'll walk you through it, and you'll do
just fine.) My first one was a folding camping shovel, but I've
since opted for a regular garden trowel. It's smaller, sturdier,
and travels well, tied to my pack with twine.

Citronella Candles

Bugs are simply going about their business of living and have
no interest in cute girls with their legs exposed. Repeat this
five hundred times, and maybe you won't need bug spray or
citronella candles. It doesn't work for me. Camping candles
come in tins with lids for safely packing, but any candles will

work. For a few bucks, they not only keep mosquitoes away but also provide camp ambience.

Cloth Gloves

Even if my muscles are up to a task, my hands sometimes object. They fancy themselves dainty types. Cloth work gloves are great for breaking up branches, getting a grip on rocks, gathering wood, pot holding, and preventing rope burn. They're my $2 insurance that my hands can pull off anything that callused hands can, minus the calluses.

Duct Tape

If you've ever mended sneakers, hemmed a dress in a hurry, or owned a duct-tape wallet, you know it's capable of amazing things. Think made-for-television kidnapping movies. No, don't think about that. Think tent, tarp, and backpack repairs. Just bring a *small* roll; duct tape is heavy.

First Aid Kit

This is one thing you'll have to head to a camping store to find. You could build your own. But by the time you run around finding everything and repackaging it for the trail, you could have bought an inexpensive camper's kit and moved on to playing doctor. A small trail kit is worth the $20 and the convenience. A decent one should include all the basics, such as ibuprofen, aspirin, antihistamine, bandages, antibiotic ointment, antiseptic towelettes, and moleskin. Don't forget to add any of your preferred remedies that might not be included. Rolaids, echinacea, cranberry tablets, and aloe lotion are my necessary additions.

Flashlights

Faulty flashlights are not uncommon; bring two or three. They'll guide you to a safe place to pee, stop a sneaky spider in its tracks, and light up the tent for late-night antics. (Most tents have some mechanism for hanging a flashlight from the ceiling.) Flashlights need batteries—either use a tester or change all batteries every time you set off on a trip. And always bring a few extra—someone will worship you for being prepared.

Matches and Lighters

Spark it up, girl—a capable camper is always prepared with a few ways to start a fire. Matchbooks are an obvious, lightweight choice. But matchboxes are more water-resistant, and also cute, covered in glittery collages. (Personalized matchboxes make perfect trip favors.) Stash some lighters, too—put one in your pocket, one in your toiletry pouch, and one in your pack. Lighters walk off just as fast in the woods as they do in smoky bars. My favorite thingamajig for a third alternative is a magnesium fire starter, available in camping stores. Strike the hunk of magnesium on one end with a knife to sprinkle flammable shavings, then strike the flint on the other end to spark up the bits. For less than $10 you've got a pocket survival tool and a neato parlor trick.

Paper Towels

I'm a sucker for their absorbent goodness, and now that I'm a grown-up I can use as many as I like without hearing how much each sheet costs. It's nice to have something to wipe your hands on other than your pants in the backcountry. One roll usually works for a few people on a weekend trip. Squash the roll a few times to separate the cardboard from the paper, and then work and wiggle it out from the center. Now flatten the roll for easy packing. Even though used paper towels also make good fire starters, conscientious campers prefer reusable bandanas and dishrags for cleaning up. Bring a few of those too—they can wash dishes, dry bodies, and strain water.

Plastic Bags

The future is in plastics. Well, I don't know about that, but I do know if you leave half this list at home, make sure you've at least got the plastic bags. Tear three appropriate holes in a garbage bag and you've got a poncho. Keep a dry stash of toilet paper in a grocery bag hung from a branch. Store leftovers away from the powerful snouts of forest dwellers in a ziplock. Plastic bags are light and reusable, so I don't skimp on them. Their usefulness is unparalleled. Waterproof your pack with a garbage bag. Protect your butt from wet ground. Clean up and pack out all your trash. Nest clothes and toiletries in grocery bags to stay organized and dry. Before you go, transfer boxed food to baggies to save on weight and space in your pack. Marinate vegetables and pack out smelly waste in ziplocks. I'm known to go overboard, but each trip I bring about five lawn-sized garbage bags, five grocery bags, and ten ziplock bags of various sizes.

Making peace. *Bandana crowd . . . Gore-Tex types*—I'm probably not building friendships in camping circles by using these phrases. Truth is, I've learned a lot from this skilled, dedicated crowd. Bandanas really are vital in the backcountry. And Gore-Tex, though some folks take their love of it to the extreme, is nifty because it lets sweat out but doesn't let rain in. ☙

Pocketknife

Whether you're an Iron Chef or a Crocodile Hunter, a basic pocketknife is an asset in the backcountry—to trim ends of rope, clean your nails, core an apple, whittle a unicorn. If you can score one with a corkscrew, can opener, and maybe a cuticle pusher too, you'll be ready for anything. But as fun as they are to play with, a good pocketknife can be expensive (most start at around $30). Any small kitchen knife is a totally acceptable alternative. Just don't forget a corkscrew and can opener too. And before you buy, or steal stuff from your kitchen, check with the men in your life. Pocketknives are the quintessential manly present, even for metropolitan dudes. My dad's junk drawer rattled with eight abandoned models before I cleaned it out.

Rope

Just think of all the kinky things you'll be able to do with rope once you learn to tie knots like a foul-mouthed sailor. Rope is a camper's good friend. You'll need it to tie items onto your pack for easier travel, make a clothesline, hang food out of the reach

Speaking of civilization. Next to *cell phone* on the GLOK list is a note from Jen, "I have a good one, and I'm bringing a colleague's number from Lexington who will rescue us (me) if need be!" There must be few cell towers in the Daniel Boone National Forest, because no one got reception on that trip. There are obvious emergency situations that can be more easily solved with a cell phone, but most times in the backcountry you'd have better luck with a bullhorn. Be prepared for few, if any, signal bars in the wild. ❦

of hungry scavengers, and rig a tarp. Look for braided, pinky-thick, nylon rope; it's easiest to work with. And bring along a few lengths—one at least twenty feet long and a few shorter pieces. I also carry a small spool of twine—it's light and suitable for small jobs.

Watch

If you need to meet your new boyfriend's parents or make it to your high school reunion on Sunday afternoon and you plan on hiking out on Sunday morning, bring a watch with an alarm. If you have no such appointments, why not go without? Detaching yourself from all the symbols and demands of civilization—time being just about the most niggling—is bizarrely rousing. Your body will take over and let you know when you're awake, tired, or hungry, without being told by Sony.

Whistle

Get out in the middle of nowhere, slide that sucker between your lips, and blow hard—whistle therapy. If necessary, whistles can also be used to startle humans and animals alike. Chances are you won't need it to scare off bears or perverts, but you can still use it to play Vengeful Gym Teacher.

Let No Carabiner Stand in Your Way

Camping gear is undeniably cool. Tents, sleeping bags, backpacks, and purifiers are all ingenious, portable solutions for straightforward challenges. In less than eight minutes you can have a comfy, cute, sturdy roof overhead—apartment hunting has never been that clear-cut. Need a place to rest your head? A sleeping bag makes for a pleasant night's stay anywhere— from a forest to a porch to an ex-boyfriend's bedroom floor. How often, in the city, do we brandish plastic and rope in the face of inclement weather? When it rains I usually stay home, call a cab, or get soaked because I forgot my umbrella. Flip through a camping catalogue; there are even neater thingamabobs and doodads to pull off all kinds of tasks. And there are also amazing guides and stores offering extensive how-to's and materials to build all your own equipment from scratch. Buy every contraption and gizmo your wallet will allow, or invent your own sleeping bag filled with shredded hoodies. Follow my pared-down lead, or let it give you courage to define your personal camping style.

A few years ago I got the notion I wanted to learn to sew. I researched definitive retro sewing guides, drooled over the revamped T-shirts I saw in sewing blogs, spent way too much

The countess of camping courage. Grandma Emma Gatewood was the first woman to hike the entire length of the Appalachian Trail, from Maine to Georgia, alone. It was 1955, and she was sixty-seven. The mom of eleven read about it in a magazine and on a whim set off carrying a blanket, raincoat, shower curtain, cup, and rations, with a pair of Keds on her feet. She must have taken to camping, because she did it two more times before she died. Still, like the best of us, she wasn't above a little complaining. "For some fool reason, they always lead you right up over the biggest rock to the top of the biggest mountain they can find." ❦

on fabric I loved, and begged my roommate to let me use her sleek new machine. When I finally sat down to make something, I was paralyzed. I couldn't even sew a pillowcase. I had put so many steps between me and the stupid skirt I wanted to make, I couldn't sew a damn thing. If my bobbin-winding goddess grandmother hadn't stepped in, I might not be turning basmati rice bags into tote bags today. She sat me down at her reliable old workhorse with a pile of fabric scraps and forced me to put my foot to the pedal.

At best I'm a mediocre seamstress, but I am proficient in self-sabotage. I know lots of fabulous ladies who are very talented at compiling overwhelming lists of things that must get done before moving on to the really good stuff—so talented, that they never *get* to the good stuff. We don't need to first tiptoe into our boss's office to ask for a raise, start a savings account, buy the best gear, take a course on understanding the gear, and lose weight to be better able to use the gear, all just to get a little primitive reprieve. Girls, gather up what you can *now* and head for the hills.

❖   ❖   ❖   ❖   ❖

And don't leave all your festive frocks and pampering products home. Getting primitive doesn't mean denying yourself everything you love. Play primal vixen or green goddess—tailor your camping style by starting with a thorough packing list. Chapter 4 offers up my packing methods for an imaginary trip and pointers for fitting it all into a pack.

Make Like a Snail

*What to bring, what to leave home,
and how to squeeze it all into a backpack.*

When I pack for a vacation, even an overnight stay, it's a drama, occasionally a melodramatic one. I'm always running late. And unless it's been planned and approved the night before, I can have a very emotional time deciding what to wear. Added to that, I'm a procrastinator. All this means that when I'm trying to get out the door for a trip, I'm frantic. I'm plagued by pimples, scrutinizing myself in the mirror repeatedly, and at the very last second grabbing multiple outfit possibilities, blow dryer, iron, and every bit of makeup I own and stuffing them in my round, brown vintage Samsonite. If the whole event were filmed with time-lapse photography, there would be a blur of hair engulfed in growing heaps of clothing, sprinkled with intermittent periods of a fleshy ball writing on the floor. It is a wonder I get anywhere.

I guess it's more of a shocker that I manage to camp. I'm the first to agree. I'd be the first to toss in the towel and scream for mercy. The irony here is a testament to why camping is actually just what the doctor should order for us overworked, overanalyzed, overly perfect city gals. The backcountry is the only place I've found where the world as I know it, the one I fret over, the very one that turns me into the manic packer does not exist. All the petty worries swimming around our pretty overachiever heads are made null and void by the simple lack of civilization as we know it. I cringe at the thought of being caught with only a suitcase full of parent-visiting clothes to choose from when confronted with a night of down-home dive bar pool, but being caught in the wild without a poncho is more like an interesting challenge than a trauma. Preparedness is rule number one of camping packing, but it's preparedness of another sort, a whole different animal—a less accessorized, more no-nonsense, much less paranoid animal.

Packing for a camping trip is about ensuring you are able to meet basic needs, not all those other nagging intangibles that induce the desperation of packing three pair of jeans, two types of foundation, four hair-taming products, and a flattening iron just to visit some friends. In the backcountry all the trappings of cool, markers of success, and proof of city savvy

Mirror, mirror. Liberate yourself from looking. It was a long time before I gave up on bringing a mirror into the backcountry; now I look forward to camping trips because they're mirror-free. I don't know how much of my lifetime I spend looking at my own reflection, but I do know it can't hurt to spend a little less. And when I get really desperate to check on my cowlick, I sneak a peek in a pool of water. ❧

will melt away—maybe not immediately, but they won't fit in a pack and there won't be much use for them anyway. Camp packing demands that we exercise the parts of our brains untainted by any thought of the last time we got a pedicure. For the organizer, it's an excuse to make lists and then later revise them. For the crafty, it's a time to experiment and invent new uses for common objects. For the thrifty, it's an opportunity to streamline and lighten the load. Figuring out what you'll need and what will best suit those needs is a recipe you'll perfect. Fitting and balancing it all in a neat package you'll support with your back is a unique physical and mental challenge. It's a time to question wants and needs and an experiment in scaling down. Packing for a camping trip is perfectly suited for us multitasking resourceful little city mice.

Break It Down

First things first—make a list. Type it, scribble it, illustrate it, make a collage, or use stickers. Whatever you do, first carefully think it through, and second follow all the rational thoughts you've managed to work out. Exercise that brain to make sure you cover everything, then don't allow mindless indulgent straying. There won't be a Store24 out there for the lighter you forgot, but you won't even make it to your site if you bring two of everything you think you might need.

Like a sourdough starter, you'll write your first list and then keep it handy to build upon and make notes later. For example, next to *tequila* on my Kentucky list is scribbled "Didn't need.

Whiskey better." Truth be told, I sometimes forget to revisit my list back at home when all I want to do is shower and check email. But that's a lazy mistake. Revising your list while your memory is fresh is the key to mastering the art of creature comfort on the trail. Your list will evolve as you make new discoveries and refine your camping style. My very first trip list didn't include baking soda, duct tape, or mouthwash—three things that always make the cut now. Campers all have their own ways of rationalizing what they need and how much of it to bring. Through experience you'll discover what suits you best, but you're bound to miscalculate sometimes. You'll tote things in that never make it out of the pack and leave essential items behind—both will lead to useful lessons and great stories. On a trip to Florida, I left the spoons neatly tucked away in their proper drawer at home. In a

True confessions. When talk of the GLOK camping trip first began, a certain person suggested a certain other person wouldn't be a very good camper because of her penchant for Manolo Blahnik's. The resulting uprising was quelled, and we all discovered that a love for expensive kitten heels wasn't going to stop this girl. The paraphernalia we rely on to define ourselves is stripped away in the backcountry, freeing us to transform into whatever we dream up. While the rest of us hung back at camp, the accused crawled under bushes with a flashlight in her mouth to gather our much-needed and scarce kindling. On the way back to the car, with cell phone reception happily restored, she was the first to check her voice mail and the only one of us with a message from the makeup counter at Barneys. Isn't the paradox beautiful? ❧

stroke of ingenuity we made do with broken seashells. Spooning rice and beans to our mouths with a shared corner of smoothly worn conch was both a bit barbaric and slightly sexy. On the other hand, things could have been very uncomfortable, perhaps violent, if I had forgotten the bug spray.

I divide my list into six areas: Gear, Clothes, Toiletries, Kitchen, Food & Booze, and Miscellaneous. It's obvious what goes where, but I admit the *Miscellaneous* column always gets a lot more action than it should, because I use it as a catchall for anything I can't place or might forget. Weather, location, length and type of trip, whims, mood, and moon phases are all carefully considered before every trip, but the bare list of necessities is fairly consistent. The main rule, the big one, is to think about each day's needs before adding anything to the list. Make a chart breaking down the days of your trip and roughly allocate clothes, supplies, food, and booze for each. I even go as far as to divide the days up into morning, afternoon, and night. This

Miso Scared. I read a disarming trip report of a young woman's first solo outing. She spent the night before her big adventure packing and unpacking her bag, adjusting items to create the best load. All that hard work and then she left her food pouch on the bed. She discovered this on the fifth mile of her hike when reaching for an apple. In a testament to her forum moniker, struttin_owless, she lasted two days on water and a few Power Bars. This story, unlike my seductive seashell romp, incites panic in my miso soup-loving heart and reminds me to be a good little list maker and thoroughly anal scout. 🐾

is the only way to ensure I don't overpack, and it still fails me. For example, I have the pants I'm bringing for days one and two, then the pants I want for day three, but then I secretly (as if I can *secretly* keep it from myself) throw in one more pair.

Start big, but be willing to whittle. The four T-shirts, five rolls of toilet paper, and three novels you simply need, you'll need a lot less when you try on your pack, and then even less after hiking a few minutes. If there was a math equation for packing, X would be the length of the trip and Y would be how far the hike is to the campsite. (D would be something like the Don't-want-to-break-my-back-but-still-want-to-have-fun quotient.) Don't worry, I hate math too. I'll talk you through my deep dark organizational processes, reveal my checklists, and show you how to squeeze it all into 3,500 cubic inches. As you actually do it, everything will make sense. I promise.

Wilderness Wear

Gear is easy—all my camping stuff patiently waits in a closet for its next trip. Grub (and in my camp, booze) is so essential we'll need a separate chapter to discuss it. So let's chat about clothes. Visit a camping outfitter, flip on the Discovery Channel, spy on campers—you'll see drab-colored fabric cut into shapes almost completely devoid of any interesting style. I don't have a reserve of sensible duds for camping. I enjoy looking cute. I like bright colors. I love vintage. Why should this change just because I'm in the backcountry? I may not wear my old cherished Levi's, but I still want to feel fabulous when

I'm out there. A-line skirts, striped knee-highs, and tube tops have all made it on my treks. If sparkly things make you smile, take an old pair of flip-flops and cover them with glitter. Try out that wild backless T-shirt you're afraid to wear in public. Or create your own Xena-wear for tracking sparrows.

Let's play pretend. I've heard of a beautiful spot in Maine where you can hike in ten miles to a towering secret waterfall. This place is my Valhalla. I keep talking about it but never seem to get there. I've romanticized the hell out of it, so it's probably been turned into a waterpark by now. Anyway, let's imagine I'm going there and it's early July. For a three-day excursion from Friday to Sunday, here's what I'd pack.

First I'd assign a pair of pants for Friday and Saturday. By Sunday I'd need something fresh to change into, so I'd assign one more pair of pants or maybe a skirt. Pants are essential for hikes from camp; they protect your legs from thorns, ticks, and poison ivy. Skirts, on the other hand, are easy and breezy loungewear. They're like my camp housedress; I always bring one along. Tank tops and T-shirts are small and light, so I pack a fresh one for each day. Toss in a long-sleeve shirt and maybe a light hoodie too—outside the city limits even summer

Go team! Nothing raises morale like handmade presents. Like your Thursday night bowling league, troops look hot in matching personalized shirts. All you need are plain cotton T-shirts, iron-on paper, a computer, and a printer. My favorites: The Squirrel Sisters and Bullfrog Counters Club. ❧

nights can get chilly. The coziest, softest, dreamiest pajamas are a must—pamper yourself after a day tramping around the woods. Who wants to sleep in anything that touched dirt and bugs? Don't forget a change of undies for every day and a supportive bra for serious hiking and climbing. And when you're not busy being active, you have a license to go braless in the backcountry. Socks are nice to have in abundance—high socks are needed for hiking, clean socks are comforting after a long day, and warm socks are the secret ingredient to a good night's sleep. Shoes, on the other hand, are heavy—we've got no choice but to pare down, drastically. You'll need one pair of supportive shoes or sneakers for hiking and a pair of flip-flops or sandals for kicking around camp. At five in the morning I'm not capable of tying my shoes, and going barefoot among the crickets to find a spot to pee is not an option. Flip-flops or sandals are also good for feeling around on the bottom of river-beds and lakes. Speaking of rivers and lakes, don't leave home

The truth about boots. I know I've said it before, but I'll say it again. You don't have to make a huge investment to camp. I always try to find the cheap, uncomplicated alternative (when it comes to camping, at least). Cave women gathered food all year long in handmade animal-hide slippers. I have a pair of $45 sneakers I bought four years ago and those are the ones I still wear today. If you'd like to get a pair of hiking boots, just be sure to try them on first. Sturdy boots with serious soles can weigh you down and make it hard to maneuver. A lightweight trail shoe or sneaker is perfect for beginner hikers. ❖

without a bathing suit. My most memorable trips involve a dip in natural water after a long sweaty day in the dirt.

Accessorizing is up to you—if you always wear a belt, bring a belt. If you get chilly at night, sleep in a knit cap. Tailor this list to suit your style and your needs. My hair becomes a knotted greasy disaster when I go camping, so I always bring a cowboy hat and a few bandanas. A hat with a wide brim is your first line of defense against the sun, and bandanas are handy multiuse accessories. Think strainer, wash rag, and potholder. Sunglasses are always helpful, but they're essential on beach or desert trips. At the seashore you can scale down—you'll end up wearing just your bathing suit and a cover-up almost every day. In the desert, where the sun is more intense, you'll need full coverage, and at night it can be so cold you'll need sweats. In spring and autumn, layering is the trick to happy camping. When weather's unpredictable it helps to be able to add and shed as needed. The GLOK swore by their long johns for our November outing. These are excellent cool-weather camping garb and look adorable under skirts in urban winters. Rain tends to sneak up on me, so I always stash a lightweight windbreaker or poncho with a hood in my pack.

Back to my Maine fantasy. Here's what my clothing schedule might look like:

FRIDAY
Day   Cargo pants, hot pink tank, gray socks, sneakers
Night Gray hoodie, white T-shirt, black pajama bottoms, gray socks

SATURDAY

Day   Cargo pants, Willie Nelson T-shirt, brown socks, sneakers

Night   Gray hoodie, white T-shirt, black pajama bottoms, white socks

SUNDAY

Day   Jeans, yellow tank top, pink socks, sneakers

Add to that a cotton skirt and fresh T-shirt for loafing, tall socks for extra protection on hikes, flip-flops, a long-sleeve T-shirt, three pair of panties, a cowboy hat, a few bandanas, my poncho, and, of course, my brown bikini. Isn't minimalism fun?

Untamed Toiletries

Space and weight are still factors, but we all know our favorite products are available in sample sizes and can easily be smuggled into any venue. I've applied makeup in the car (while driving), under my desk, and in bathroom stalls where my only reflection was in the stainless steel toilet paper dispenser. The big question is, do we really need our beloved products out there? Or better, how many of our beloved products are we willing to leave at home? While hiking through a beautiful sandstone ravine, sur-

---

Any hat, headband, or clip is camouflage for bad camping hair. But braids are especially nice for taming primitive hair—when you take them out your hair will be wavy and willowy. Instant earth goddess. ❤

rounded by exotic vegetation, will you even think of your hair-smoothing serum? How about later that night, staring into the mesmerizing campfire built by your very hands—will you need mascara? My thesis, my whole angle, what I desperately want to convince you of is you do not have to leave behind all the girly, decadent stuff you love. I simply will not camp without pressed powder—it just makes me feel whole, my face silky, and my complexion smooth. But—incongruously, I know—I also want you to embrace the opportunity to experience yourself without the things you're convinced you need. I never indulge in foundation when I'm in the backcountry, even though I wear it every other day, without fail. When I go camping I get to flaunt my flawed skin in all its blotchy glory. It's my damn skin—look at it! And while I may leave behind the products I'm a slave to in the real world, I've found uses in the backcountry for goods I'd never dreamed of using. Dr. Bronner's and other natural liquid soaps are biodegradable and versatile. The peppermint-scented variety is not only body wash and detergent, but toothpaste too. Cornstarch is a dry shampoo for ladies plagued, like me, by grease—rub some on your roots, leave in for about ten minutes, and brush out. Baking soda is the wonder stuff. I've worked it into my at-home routine too—mixed with face wash it creates a perfectly gritty scrub. On the trail, baking soda deodorizes trash bags; scrubs pots, faces, and teeth; and when mixed with a few drops of water becomes a soothing paste for rashes and stings.

I also never camp without baby powder and baby wipes—both essential for keeping things fresh down below. Hand sanitizer is helpful if water is scarce. Mouthwash is a must, and so is your preferred birth control if you want to play Tarzan and Jane. And to spend any time in the great outdoors without sunscreen is reprehensible. A moisturizer with sunscreen kills two (origami) birds with one stone.

So what do I leave home? My hair actually looks better when I try not to tame it, so I ditch the hairbrush. And although it breaks my heart, I leave behind the electric toothbrush. It has no problem holding a charge, but it's heavy and there's something about phallic, white, vibrating things that don't feel right in the backcountry. Lip balm, pressed powder, and tweezers are the only three items I allow myself from my beloved makeup bag. (Without a mirror I can't work on my eyebrows, but tweezers are a must for splinters and [gasp] ticks.) And this doesn't mean I don't leave that bag in the car for a quick post-camping touch-up.

Finally, don't leave home without the toilet paper. I always bring too much, but I have a healthy digestive tract. About one roll for two people on a weekend trip should be sufficient. Same as with paper towels, work the cardboard center out and flatten the rolls for easier packing. I'm also a firm believer in the wisdom of *The Hitchhiker's Guide to the Galaxy*, at least when applied to camping—always bring a towel. Depending on how much of a traditionalist you want to be, you could bring a chamois or a camping towel. They're super-absorbent and light. I opt for a small bath towel because I often end up turning it into a pillow.

The trick with toiletries is devising lightweight, space-saving ways to pack them. You may have heard of hardcore campers who peel labels, saw handles, and trim centimeters off of packaging in attempts to lighten their packs. I'll do anything to make room for a bottle of wine, but being that practical is more hassle than it is worth. Be good to your back, but don't drive yourself nuts. Buy travel sizes. Repackage liquids like soap and moisturizer in small water bottles. Ditch the bulky packaging on baby wipes and stuff them into a ziplock bag. Campers love their ziplocks. Baby powder, cornstarch, baking soda—when in doubt, bag it.

Back to that trip to Maine; here's what I would bring from the toiletry department:

- Water bottle filled with Dr. Bronner's peppermint soap
- Ten baby wipes folded up in a ziplock
- Travel-size baby powder
- Travel-size lotion with sunscreen
- Travel-size hand sanitizer
- Travel-size mouthwash
- Birth control (an ample stash of condoms, in my case)

There's no such thing as tasty underarms. There was a dirty rumor on the GLOK trip about bears that like the smell of girls' deodorant. Bugs might, but bears prefer the smell of leftover cheese sandwiches to powder fresh scent. The only reason I don't bring deodorant is because I relish any excuse to smell like a trucker. Your Secret will have to work double-time out there, and chances are it won't stand up to the challenge anyway. Leave it in the car along with a fresh change of clothes so the ride home doesn't stink. ❧

- Baking soda, about ten tablespoons in a ziplock bag
- Cornstarch, about ten tablespoons in a ziplock bag
- Pressed face powder
- Lip balm
- Tweezers
- One roll of toilet paper
- Toothbrush
- Towel

Primitive Packing

Ever set your suitcase up on one of those convenient hotel stands? Eight P.M. rolls around, it's time to shower and get ready for a night on the town. You think you might get lucky, so you dig in the suitcase pocket for your razor. After your shower, a squirt of something sultry is in order. You know you rolled up perfume in

Toothbrush tutorial. When it comes time to brush your teeth in the wild, you may find you don't know where to begin. It's an odd sensation—did you ever think you'd forget how to brush? Here's my favorite method: Pour potable water into your camp cup—about half a cup should do. Put a dollop of your chosen tooth scrub on your brush. This can be a messy sight—grab a paper towel and take a few steps away from camp. Dip the brush in the cup to get it wet. Brush away. Spit into the paper towel. Take a swig of water from your cup. Swish and spit. Swirl your brush around in the cup to clean it off. Scatter the wastewater. Wipe off with a clean corner of the paper towel and toss it in the trash when you're done. Voilà—primitive pearly whites. 🐾

a sock, but which one? And where are those stockings? No stockings. Okay, maybe a quick touch-up on your nail polish. Nail polish, where would that be? Shit, did you bring heels? Oooh, there's the nail polish. But the heels, still missing. The suitcase isn't that big. Dump the damn thing out on the bed. If I packed for camping as poorly as I usually do, it would be a disaster. Dumping everything out to look for a flashlight is not an option out there, because I don't like twigs tangled up in my towel and leaves stuck to my socks. Things must be placed reasonably, with both balance and timing in mind. For example, keep your tent close to the top because it will probably be the first thing you need when you get to camp. Sneak an apple into an outside pocket for an emergency snack. Don't put all the heavy stuff on the right side unless you like limping.

Glorious delayed gratification. This is my secret recipe for a heavenly back-to-reality shower. The four most important qualities of a proper post-camping shower are *long, hot, thorough,* and *prepared.* Now is not the time to discover you're out of seaweed face scrub or low on your favorite shea body butter. When I say *long,* I mean a half an hour for bathing and at least twenty minutes before and after for grooming—tweezing, trimming, lotioning, clipping, and possibly painting. By *hot,* I mean my body is actually red when I towel off. And *thorough* means my toothbrush is begging for mercy, and I do my best shampoo-girl impression for my locks. To complete the pampering, I *prepare* a cup of something warm and cue up *Buffy* in the DVD player so when I emerge from the shower, I can languish, primp, sip, and smile. ❧

There are lots of experts out there preaching about packing. Many of these experts have contrary opinions. And many are men who have very different bodies and capabilities. Most are a tad too stringent for my taste. Keep in mind, it is just packing and it is a vacation. First, before you even unzip the pack, organize your supplies by category. If you live in close quarters like me, cover the kitchen table, coffee table, sewing table, and floor with camping paraphernalia. Now you can go down your checklist and review everything you plan to bring. It's also easier to subpack related items together in smaller bags if it's all laid out first. Some campers invest in stuff sacks for this. I just use grocery or ziplock bags. Put toiletries in one bag and socks, undies, and party supplies in others. Have a bag for every category, or let supplies roam free—be as meticulous as you like. Passengers have been known to push aside a foot of crap to sit in the backseat of my car. Thanks to camping I get to pretend I'm an everything-in-its-place-and-a-place-for-everything person in short manageable spurts. If you already are one of those you have a leg up. Organization is queen in backpack packing, and weight distribution is the court jester.

So what gets filed under miscellaneous? Maps, guides, cards, pens, camera. Usually party supplies—tape recorder, ukulele, Frisbee, water gun, book. There are no rules—a security blanket, lucky paper clip, binoculars. The one thing that never gets crossed off my Miscellaneous list is my journal. Even if I'm not inspired to write or draw, I always have a place to play hangman and paper to help start the fire. ❧

Now comes the challenge of squeezing it all into the pack, without pulling your hair out first. The basic rule of proper weight distribution is to keep the heaviest weight toward the rear and lower third of the pack, near the small of your back. This will keep your center of gravity low and close, without pulling you down or pulling the pack away from you. Try to place weight evenly on both the right and left sides of the pack so you're not yanked in one direction or the other. You may end up taking everything out and starting fresh. That's okay. Sometimes I repack my bag three times before it feels right.

Lay the pack open on the floor. Start out with a soft layer along the back, the part that comes in contact with your spine. A hoodie or towel work great as padding. Along the bottom try to fit your sleeping bag or a tightly rolled blanket. It doesn't always work—remember you can always store your bed on the outside of the pack. Try stuffing a bag of clothes in the bottom instead. The goal is to create a shelf on which to rest heavy stuff—booze, food, toiletries. Flashlights, flip-flops, and paper towels can flank the sides. Moderately heavy items can be supported up top by your shoulders, as long as you center them close to your body. Fill in gaps with socks, bags of dry food, or soft things that can be crushed, like tank tops. Keep fragile items toward the outside or

Plan a packing party. From kitchen supplies to toiletries to the tent—lots of gear is shared by the group. Designate a troop clubhouse and meet up to pack together before you go. This way you can divvy, ration, and commiserate in good company. 🐾

in exterior zipper pockets. Stuff the tent on top and tie the poles to the outside. A kitchen pot and cup also travel well tied on. I fit what kitchen supplies I can in my pack, but I often carry another shoulder bag that houses my traveling pantry.

Just because these suggestions sound great on paper doesn't mean they always translate to the field. Do what works, and make sure you're comfortable.

Time to zip up and give it a try. Lift up your pack and rest it on your knee before tossing it over your shoulder. Have a buddy help you hoist and center it on your back. Strap in—pull the shoulder, chest, and hip straps snug to your body where it's easier to bear the load. When I heave my pack up off the ground, toss it over my back, and strap in, if I don't then fall backward, lean sideways, lurch forward, or pinch a nerve, I throw my hand up in the air for a little victory fist waving. Carrying a pack isn't easy—expect to ache and possibly moan—but it also shouldn't be painful. The general rule is a pack shouldn't weigh more than 25 or 30 percent of your body weight. For me that's just under

Rest and stop. If you discover you're overburdened once you're already on the trail, you still have options. First, take lots of breaks. There's no shame in needing a rest. Take off your pack and sit for five minutes. Or take a minute's breather by bending over and letting your back be a table for your pack—it actually feels good. Reconsider your campsite. Save the long hike for later and cut it short this time. There are always plenty of places to camp in the wild. Stick a bit closer to the car than planned. Next time you'll be ready to tackle the long haul. ❧

forty pounds. Some campers suggest taking a trial hike with a full pack. It's great advice if you've got the time. If not, stick to the 30 percent rule and walk around the house with it on. How does it feel? Be honest. Imagine carrying it for one hour, or two. If you've properly planned the trip, you won't be hiking an unmanageable distance. If you're trying to conquer a steep or lengthy hike, sacrifice some goods. The reward of an intense hike is in pulling it off. That kind of trip doesn't really call for wine. How about switching to a flask of whiskey? A common culprit of a monstrous pack is too many clothes, or poor consolidation of toiletries. Leave some fruit behind. Although I love apples with my cheese, if my pack hurts I'll have to go without. There's always some way to cut down on weight without forgoing happiness. It's not easy to distill your wants and needs down to a package you're responsible for carrying on your back. But it's a revealing exercise, and, truth is, it's fun. You'll be the model of independence and adventure. A modern mollusk—with a silky moisturizer, a good book, and, if you're lucky, a cup of cabernet. Cheers.

🐾 🐾 🐾 🐾 🐾

Soup's on! From campfire coffee and biscuits to the Post-camping-Trip Eating Extravaganza, chapter 5 offers everything you need to know about primitive feasts. You'll pack rations that travel well, build a simple backcountry kitchen, learn the basics of fire cooking, borrow some of my favorite recipes, and fearlessly invent your own camp menu.

Hungry Like a Wolf, Thirsty Like a Fish

Building a traveling kitchen, stocking a primitive pantry, and preparing tasty camp feasts.

More often than I'd like to admit, I roll out of bed already thinking about what's for dinner. Tastes of tangy lemongrass soup, fleshy injera bread, and tuna subs stacked with pickles dance in my head, and my hips betray the path of my culinary travels. Food and booze equal my happiness. Though you may normally eat like a bird, be prepared to devour like a wolf on the trail. Blame the exercise, the fresh air, or the sun—the backcountry works appetites into a frenzy. Some of the greatest camping moments are those when you collapse, lusciously plump and soused, after a long day outside, or when you perk back up in the brisk morning air to something warm and hearty. Camp cooking calls for pared-down tools, resourceful preparation, a taste for invention, and at times a yogi's balance. And camp eating is just plain fun. There's a good reason that dads are obsessed with barbecue and lovers love a picnic. Cooking in the great outdoors satiates an almost primal urge, and noshing under the sun and stars is romantic even if it's on a patch of Astroturf.

Don't consider yourself a foodie? Camp cooking will provoke your edible experimentation. Novice cooks are more comfortable in the wilderness, without all those intimidating kitchen gadgets, and experts make new discoveries venturing into unfamiliar territory. My camp tastes have evolved since I began, and my menu still changes with every trip. On my first outing, breakfast was a granola bar, and dinner was a box of Goya rice. Now I find bliss in a drowsy breakfast of pear pancakes with whiskey-spiked coffee, and decadence in a dinner of cheesy polenta bake with roasted corn on the cob, washed down with spicy Mexican hot cocoa. In the backcountry you'll transform simple ingredients into unusual dishes, try things you might never consider at home, and stir up chow perfectly suited for your inner vagabond.

Popular camp fare usually tends toward one of two extremes. Some sticklers still favor the flavorless porridge and tough jerky approach, but many savvy campers campaign for the delicious

Lazy noodles. Like most college freshmen I developed an unhealthy addiction to Top Ramen and was surprised to find it's also notorious among campers. It scores points for being lightweight and versatile—dress it up in limitless ways. Ditch the high-sodium chemicals in the little silver packet for your own spice combination, and slurp up those wily noodles sans guilt. ❧

(but slightly incongruous) dehydration method. This group would be the sure winners in a high school student council race. Their persuasive platform insists you can eat anything you want. Kung pao chicken, steak fajitas, sloppy joes, even tuna casserole is fair game. There's no mystery at work. The secret is in an $80 dehydrator. Prepare meals at home as usual and then shrivel them up with electricity and heat. At camp, rehydrate with hot water and maybe a few additions for doctoring. The lure of a gourmet meal could drag me naked across a bed of nails, but something about this method is peculiar. On the trail we don't brush our teeth the same way we do at home or poop the same way or sleep the same way. There's very little we do the same out there. So why would we expect, or even want, to eat the same as usual? A BLT at a greasy spoon is just right for some times, lasagna in Little Italy for others, and backcountry dishes can be uniquely backcountry and still delicious. Using lightweight and fundamental ingredients in daring combinations, you can please indulgent appetites and still play mountain girl, minus contraptions and complications. Call it down-home, rustic, or earthy—your camp cuisine will be tasty.

Nomadic Dishware and Wayfaring Spoons— Building a Traveling Kitchen

You may already own most of what you need to outfit a simple portable kitchen. Be inventive. Bake biscuits in an aluminum-foil oven. Stick a brownie in an airtight bag and dunk it in hot water for a warm, chewy treat. Strain pasta through a bandana.

Some folks favor a fancy camp cookery set, complete with whisk; others swear by a cup and a pair of chopsticks. Find your happy medium that's both cheap and efficient. My back-country kitchen—pot, plate, spoon, cup, knife, washbasin, and, of course, stove—has never left me hungry.

Turn It On

Your trusty stove will serve up a requisite cup of coffee quicker than any fire, produce lovely macaroni and cheese in the windiest conditions, and revive your soggy bones with Raspberry Zinger even when it's pouring. The elements make for inconsistent and unpredictable campfire results. Sometimes fires aren't even allowed. Think of the camp stove as your star player and the campfire as your trick shot. They play well together—prepare rice on the stove and roast onions in the fire.

A camp stove is just a burner that screws onto a fuel tank. Any middle shelf model from a camping store will suit novice campers on short, warm-weather trips. Avoid refillable liquid gas tanks—they require regular upkeep and cleaning. Cartridge stoves, with disposable tanks, are ideal for newbies. The more you pay (somewhere between $20 and $100), the lighter and sturdier your stove will be, but there's no need for fancy. My $40 model is less than four pounds with two propane canisters, and it doesn't weigh me down or disappoint my dinner guests. The biggest difference in stoves is the type of fuel they consume. Butane, propane, and blends are most common. Blends are generally praised for better burning, but the cartridges are a bit more expensive. Read up on your stove's burn time (how long it takes to use up fuel) and boil time (how long it takes to boil a quart of water). Check your fuel supply before you head out, and pack a meal that doesn't require cooking in case the fuel gods and campfire goddesses decide to take a day off.

Cook It Up

One medium soup pot can serve up all your camping meals without a glitch. He's the little pot that could—not only can he boil, he's willing to fry and sauté too. The cheapest one from my cupboard has become my constant companion. There's nothing you can't make using one pot, but it is more efficient to work with two. I recently buckled and bought a camping skillet. The skillet sautés parsnips over the fire while the pot boils soup on the stove. Camping pots and pans are usually under $20 and fold or nest for easy packing. But a household pot travels fine tied onto the back of a pack or does double duty as the armor for fragile stuff inside.

Dish It Out

Bowls are suitable for offerings, ceremonies, and spells, but plates are perfect for camping. With two sturdy plastic plates (patio dishware, not disposable style) you'll have one for chopping and one for eating. They're also good as lids to keep food warm, serving platters for entertaining, and fans to stoke

Foiled again! Don't forget plenty of aluminum foil if you plan on playing with fire and food. I always slide at least six 8 by 8-inch sheets in a book for safekeeping. 🐾

All Fired Up

Campers are a resourceful bunch. They pride themselves on devising astounding solutions for the lack of typical resources in the wild. For some, it's survival; for most, it's a MacGyver complex. Leaves, coffee cans, cardboard, rocks, dirt, and all manner of aluminum foil constructs have been used to cook up a campfire meal. The designs are worthy of their very own gallery of campy technology. Some look like 1953 visions of alien ships and others like grade-school science projects. Look to the ancients. Dabble in the mediums. Reflect heat; suspend yams; skewer spinach. But remember, fire cooking is the essence of imperfection. Things get charred or feel like they're taking a lifetime. When a speedy meal is needed to soothe savage beasts, stick with your steadfast stove. And when adventure is in the air, test your prehistoric prowess. Here are some basics of cooking over a campfire to ignite your experiments.

Successful campfire cuisine starts with the way the fire is built. Think long and slow-burning versus quick and sudden. A steady blaze for cooking can be had with careful building, consistent feeding, and a selection of hardwood. All wood is hard, you say? The heavier a wood, the longer and slower it will burn. Truth is, rarely will you get to be choosy in your wood selection. Once a fire has burned a while, any log should produce low flames and reduce to bright glowing bits perfect for cooking. Ignorant bosses, sloppy hairdressers, stinky selection of firewood—we endure. As long as you've got fire, you can cook. And the first and easiest way is the stick method. Use green (as in not snappy), thin sticks. Trim the bark off the end with a knife, creating a sharp point, and murder that marshmallow. Hold whatever you're cooking over the flames but not too close or the outside will burn while the inside stays cold. My favorite stick trick is Forest Fondue. Bring along a packet of the powdery cheese stuff from a box of macaroni and cheese. Prepare it in a pot over the stove. Have fun with spices and extra cheese. Put out a display of mushrooms, cherry tomatoes, bits of bread, and (my favorite) olives, for warming over the flames. Then take the roasted morsels for a dip in the orange goodness.

Holding dinner on the end of a stick over an open flame—does it get any more idyllic? Lapping flames are great for toasting bread and shish kebabs, but the red coals in the fire pit are more potent for cooking a whole meal. Fill up a pot or pan, cover tightly with a lid or foil, and nestle it right in there. This works for one-pot meals and you can also grill sandwiches this way—oil up the pan, fry, flip, fry. Or skip the pots. Wrap goodies in foil. And slip the packets in among the coals. Take a careful peek at their progress every so often. Corn on the cob and marinated potatoes are excellent roasted this way. Another bonus: coal cooking provides the primal pleasure of poking things with a big stick. Fiddle with the coals occasionally to feed and keep them hot.

Another surefire, but stick-free, camp cooking technique is to build a backcountry barbecue. When I started camping, I carried a heavy, smelly camping grill until it dawned on me to steal the small grate from my toaster oven. Camping grates are big affairs with folding legs, but a small one from an old hibachi works fine supported by two carefully arranged rocks. Grill, or use the grate as a burner for a pot. Or ditch the grate and just use the rocks. Place a flat rock near, but not in, the center of the fire, and let it heat up. Now you've got a backcountry burner or even a griddle. Sound crazy? Go wild—the thrill of campfire cooking is playing rogue chef.

the fire. Bowls are a challenge to pack, and a cup will suffice when the need to slurp arises. A $5 stainless-steel cup was my first official camping purchase. Hook the handle onto your pack with a carabiner for easy access and space saving. Don't be alarmed if you suddenly break out in a camper jig to the twangy clamor of your rattling cup and pot.

Spork It In

I say spoon, you say fork, and we all spork. Personally, I'm a spoon girl. Spoons are good for both shoveling and stirring grub. Feel too crude eating everything with a spoon? Indulge in a fork, but remember, fewer utensils mean less to keep track of and wash. Sporks are nifty too, but harder to find in metal. As primitive as I'm willing to get, I don't like eating with plastic. Camping stores sell titanium backpacking utensils (including sporks), but don't bother. It's cheaper (and forgivable) to borrow a few from your mom's old set and forget to give them back.

Cut It Open

Who doesn't kind of enjoy the feel of a good knife in their hand? It's like getting to be the one to write on the chalkboard in math class. A good pocketknife is costly (at least $30), and if you're obsessive like me you don't want your big investment greasy and grimy from cutting cheese. Dedicate a knife for

Measure up. Before you head out, use a measuring cup and a marking pen to transform your drinking cup into an even handier cooking tool. No mushy rice and watery soup. ❧

kitchen duties. Go all Ginsu or grab a steak knife out of the drawer—anything that can cut fruit will do. Camping knives fold up, but if you opt for plain old cutlery, improvise a sheath with a few layers of duct tape. And if you don't have a pocket-knife equipped with a can opener and a corkscrew, bring along small household or camping varieties. The frustration of an unopenable can or bottle can lead to violent acts.

And Scrub It Down

Rivers and streams are not sinks. Dirty dishes can't be washed in natural water. Food and soap contaminate the water, and its parasites contaminate you. I find the easiest way to wash my pot is to boil water in it. Then wipe out the remaining gunk with a paper towel, and let lemon juice do a natural deodorizing. To wash the regular way with soap and water, you'll need a basin (and a few old dishrags). A simple painter's bucket is a popular washbasin. Though it's a bit clumsy, it can also be used to nest kitchen supplies. I cut the top off an old collapsible water jug with a flat bottom, but you can score a light, folding sink for about $15 in any camping store. They're great for dishes but even better for an open-air foot soak beside the fire.

Know the triple-reverse valley fold? On her GLOK shopping spree, Rachel discovered a nifty novelty—nearly weightless, cheap, thin, plastic, folding bowls. Oatmeal fans should add these to their arsenal; just brush up on origami skills or pack the assembly directions. 🐾

Primitive Preparations

You don't really need a camping cookbook to impress your woodland friends with a backcountry feast. Easy camp cooking includes light ingredients that travel well—rice, broccoli, garlic, cheese, beans—and a few less practical additions for fun—a can of salsa or syrupy pears. Once you realize there's no big secret, you'll feel free to design your own menu. Pore over your cookbooks for recipes that translate to the trail or rely on common kitchen favorites. Indian dal, Southern-style fried plantains, Moroccan chickpea stew, apple turnovers, even garlic knots, can all be made out there. Choose from a camp cupboard filled with vegetables and fruit; cheese, beans, and nuts for protein; grains, like penne, couscous, and rice; and, of course, seasonings. Think differently. Solve the puzzles of weight and space. Assume you can't have pasta pesto out there? The pasta is a no-brainer, but the pesto is a snap too. There are two options. Tightly roll a few tablespoons of prepared pesto in a ziplock bag, and stash it in the freezer well before you go.

Surprise! Before I startle you with a menu that doesn't read like typical mess-hall fare, let me make an official (maybe obvious) announcement: backcountry camping does not involve coolers. Coolers and the stuff that go in them are heavy and require ice. So no coolers, no ice, and no ice cream, potato salad, hot dogs, or hamburgers. You'll have to get by without some perishable summer camp favorites and dream up substitutions for others. ❦

When it's time to leave, pack it in the middle of your pack (it'll stay cooler) in a few layers of plastic. By the time you hike in and set up camp, your pesto will be thawed for dinner. Or, improvise a primitive pesto right in your wilderness kitchen. All the basic ingredients will last unrefrigerated. Fold a few clean, dry, basil leaves in a paper towel. Throw some ground pine nuts into one bag and grated cheese in another. When you're ready for dinner, sauté them in oil with chopped garlic. Add salt and you've got rustic pesto. A crafty primitive chef coaxes the most out of staple ingredients, beguiles guests with improvised gourmet flavors, and keeps a few tried-and-true backcountry secrets up her sleeve.

Savage Stock

Most vegetables are naturals in the wild, but not all can survive the backpack crunch, and others are just too bulky. Tomatoes bruise, so go with sun-dried. Broccoli is a sturdy and versatile vegetable with real lasting power—trim off the ends to save

One for the test kitchens. Thanks to the freezer technique, the GLOK sat on the edge of a log dipping carrots into guacamole. No funny smell. No icy chunks. Just green goodness. The trick is simple: freeze temperature-sensitive stuff before you go, and it'll be perfectly thawed by the time camp is set up. It worked great with tomato paste, but I think I was asking for it with fish sticks. Plan to eat the frozen stuff on the first night, and skip anything potentially hazardous to your health, like chicken. 🐾

space. From the tiny to the robust, peppers are good travelers. Use them to add intensity or make them the heart of a dish. Bell peppers stuffed with grains and cheese seem to please most picky meat lovers. Mushrooms, particularly portabellas, are harder to pack but also cure meaty cravings. Baby carrots are an easy snack. Potatoes aren't light, but I occasionally bring a couple anyway for their filling, roasted goodness.

Some veggies are reluctant campers. Zucchini is too sensitive. Eggplant is too large. Lettuce will wilt on you. But dicing and mixing with oil, vinegar, and spices will help almost any vegetable last and cuts down on bulk too. Package the mix in an airtight bag and marinate as you hike. Vegetarians will easily adjust to camping food, but if you don't regularly get enough plant matter, maybe your trip will be a convenient colonic. Purge your system and up your vitamin intake.

Fruit has a tendency to be hefty, and smaller varieties, like grapes or cherries, often perish quickly. Citrus is a reliable camp choice—it has its own protective container, it's not too heavy, and it has lots of uses. Oranges make for interesting sauces and are tasty squeezed into water. Lemon juice deodorizes pots and pans. And limes help tequila go down. (Although I prefer natural, those lemon-shaped bottles of lemon juice hold a lot

The stinking rose is a smart gal's trail companion. Garlic is small and light. It can season just about any dish. It wards off colds and vampires (according to some mythology, anyway). It's also believed to provide strength in battle and stamina for conquering distant lands. ❧

more liquid.) Apples are a must on my camp fruit list. They're weighty, but for me a camping trip isn't a camping trip without apple and cheese sandwiches. The earthy air does something for the already rudimentary flavor. Since fruit is usually a snack (and I have a salt tooth), I find it hard to rationalize using up pack space for a big fruit stash. One orange, lemon, apple (for sandwiches), and banana (for dessert) usually fulfill my fruit fancies for a weekend.

On to the important stuff: goat, provolone, cheddar, Swiss, even those individually wrapped American imposters get my saliva going. Cheese is a magical trail treat. It's filling, substantial, protein-rich, and travels well. (I should say *most* cheeses travel well. I leave brie, blue, feta, and other stinky softies home for my post-trip cheese enjoyment.) A nibble of choice cheese feels especially luxurious in the great outdoors. Unaccustomed to eating it at room temperature? It's even tastier. One of the requirements for the GLOK trip was that each lady had to tote a new type she had never tasted. It's a revealing and delicious game. Cheese transforms grains into a whole meal, is essential to the classic heartwarming sandwich, and gives breakfast some oomph. For a three-day trip I always bring two bricks of cheese, and that doesn't even include any for sharing.

Laura was so taken with apple and cheese sandwiches, she was determined to sample every GLOK cheese variety between the bread and fruit. We had to bribe her with the promise of more apple and cheese sandwiches for breakfast to get her to share dinner with us. 🐾

As for less fatty ways to get protein—beans, beans, are good for your heart. (Don't worry, there's plenty of wide-open space.) We've been brainwashed. Beans can do a lot more than sit in a sweet brown sauce next to hot dogs. Think chili or chunky mock hummus. Cannellini fried in olive oil with garlic and broccoli makes a surprisingly authentic-tasting Italian meal. One fifteen-ounce can feeds two people. Bringing too many cans gets heavy, though, and most dried beans need to be soaked too long, but lentils are both quick-cooking and light. Nuts are also lightweight and nourishing additions to dishes. Walnuts, almonds, and sunflower seeds are great with grains—unless, like me, you polish them off right out of the bag.

Grains and pastas mingle with all this other stuff to create a complete dish. They're about equal in weight, so pick your favorite. Whole grains are healthier, but if you prefer ziti, live dangerously. In my early days as camp chef, I stuck to plain brown

What about meatheads? In typical gender hijinks, a couple on our Catskills trip packed their rations separately as a test to see what they each would deem proper sustenance. When it was time to show the goods, she unpacked whole wheat pretzels, mushrooms, rice, cheese, bread, tea, and instant soup. He laid two things on the table: a three-pound stick of pepperoni and a sharp knife. After teasing him sufficiently, we bartered our healthy fare for some zesty slivers. Dried meat doesn't fulfill like a Delmonico steak, but it is yummy. Nibble right off the stick, or slice and warm in a skillet. Canned meat—tuna, salmon, chicken, even Spam—is also a popular choice for carnivores. ❧

rice, but now I aim to coordinate related grains to create special dishes. Basmati rice for Indian recipes. Cracked wheat in stuffed peppers. Shells (always) in macaroni and cheese. Polenta for a twist on breakfast. Overly boiled sushi rice for dessert porridge. Don't forget a loaf of bread, pitas, or tortillas for sandwiches. Bread inevitably gets squished in a backpack, but a quick lunch of sandwiches leaves more time to play in the sun.

The last but extremely essential additions to your primitive pantry are seasonings and condiments ingeniously packed for the trail. My resourceful Boy Scout introduced me to handy spice packs. Prepare seasoning mixtures before you head out, and you'll have a gourmet collection of flavor to choose from in

A dash of this, just a hint of that. To make spice packs you'll need old 35mm film canisters (the clear ones are easier to label and poke with a knife), a few favorite seasonings, a small bowl, a sharp pointy knife, and a marking pen or labels. Clean out the film canisters with soap and hot water. Make sure the chemical film smell is gone, and dry them out thoroughly. Next, take stock of the meals you're planning. Try to reproduce the flavor of your favorite dish. Or just go with the spices you most commonly use. Mix pinches of each in the bowl, or be precise and use measuring spoons. Stir it up. Wet your pinkie finger and taste. When you're satisfied with the results, seal in a canister, and label with the marking pen or a sticker. Repeat as often as you'd like. I like one fiery mix, one complicated and pungent, and one that's simple and sweet. Shake it out—take an extra lid and punch holes in it with the tip of the knife, and you've got a shaker top for the trail. 🐾

the backcountry. Don't leave your beloved salt, pepper, or sugar behind. Spices are virtually weightless, so go nuts. Ziplock bags with a few tablespoons of hot sauce and maple syrup mean I don't have to suffer through breakfast. And save all those individual servings of honey, soy sauce, mustard, mayonnaise, and ketchup from take-out restaurants and fast-food joints. They are as precious in your traveling kitchen as cigarettes in prison.

Be the Julia Child of the wild. Master these time-honored tricks and spiffy solutions, then revamp, revise, and risk.

- Butter doesn't travel well, and oil can be substituted in just about every dish. My stepdad, the chef, would freak— I use vegetable oil. Olive oil makes grilled cheese taste too Mediterranean. Whichever you choose, buy a small plastic bottle or transfer to an old water bottle for traveling.

- I like to think they were thinking of campers' happiness when they invented tea bags of coffee. They're convenient and tidy, and they don't taste too shabby. Two per cup work for me, but for a stronger brew try the more expensive pods made for single-serve machines. Take cream

Mix it up. Trail mix makes campers whole again. But it's expensive, and all the store brands start to taste the same after a few trips anyway. Make your own more interesting blends. Save money. And lure a hungry lumberjack back to your tent. Spicy, sweet, salty, sour—no flavor is off limits. A camper once wowed me with a daring combination involving wasabi peas and Swedish fish. But here's my all-time favorite: almonds, white chocolate chips, vanilla-infused granola, and dried cherries. ❧

with that? Powdered milk will have to do. If you'll be adding it to recipes too, use real powdered milk, not the fake creamer stuff.

- Just add water. Instant soup is a pleasant trail pick-me-up—I have a soft spot for miso. Pudding is a popular scouting dessert. Rice and pasta mixes are great bases for bigger meals—just add vegetables and spices to dress them up. Skip the supermarket standards. There are excellent, exotic, even healthy alternatives for campers in camping-supply stores—imagine dining on instant sweet corn chowder, focaccia, and Bavarian chocolate mousse beside a babbling brook.

- It breaks my heart, but there will be no egg breaking in the backcountry. Powdered eggs, found in baking and camping specialty stores, will have to substitute for scrambled. When you taste them fried with cheese and stuffed into a warm tortilla, you'll be happy to play their fool.

- Defiled Tang is just what the astronauts ordered. Powdered drink mixes are a virtually weightless way to add zing to water. They also make decent mixers for drinks of the alcoholic persuasion.

- Don't trust those persuasive Ding Dongs. Treats are whimsical. It's easy to get carried away. Plan for one snack a day, and you'll have plenty. Cookies, crackers, candy, and fruit all make good camping snacks—just pick your poison. The one thing that doesn't hold up in a backpack: potato chips. I leave my beloved salt-and-vinegar chips home.

- Grated Parmesan cheese is the wonder camp condiment. It adds flavor and texture and provides protein, it's light, and it lasts. If you're used to the freshly grated variety, switch to the nonclumping stuff just for camping.

- Packaging is paramount. Thinking up clever ways to pack and recycle is part of the challenge of playing backcountry chef. Leave the box of aluminum foil home and fold up a few large squares for the road. Ditch the cardboard on instant mixes and write the directions directly on the bag. Store grains or premixed recipes in ziplock bags with the instructions written on them. Then reuse the bags for dirty socks, leftovers, or a leaf collection.

Irrational Rations

Rather than hiking out with a liberated load, I'm often lugging back leftover boxes, bags, and cans of food. My habits tend toward overindulgence. The only way I've found to prevent, or at least discourage, overpacking is to plan every meal. Just like you designate outfits for each day, you'll have to designate dishes. Sound too boring? It's just for packing purposes. You don't have to stand by the schedule when it comes to your cravings. How many days will you be gone for? When do you arrive and leave? Consider portions and how many mouths need feeding, then make a grocery list. Don't forget the trimmings—oil, spices, condiments, powdered milk, coffee, and tea. Break down the shopping list, and have one person deal with dinners while another masters snacks. Make use of the different sizes of ziplock bags. Small is perfect for powdered milk, medium holds cheese, and large can handle entire meals. Mix up recipes, add water to dough, and marinate right in the bags. Airtight bags are also a must to prevent leaking and transport trash home. Distribute the supplies among everyone's packs. Put heavy items in the center and fragile goods in outer pockets. The chow is often the heaviest part of the load; no one should carry it alone. Kitchen supplies can also be consolidated into one shoulder bag. Pass it back and forth like a hot potato on the trail.

The first time I calculated correctly and packed the right amount of food, I danced, bragged, and made everyone bear witness to the paltry leftovers. One apple, a few tablespoons of oil, and some spices were all that remained by midnight on our last night. I wobbled back to my tent with a smug, sleepy grin and, in a rare display of naked elation, I mooned the camp. The next morning, thanks to a thoughtful comrade, I woke to curried fried apples and we hiked out, ceremoniously crumb-free. Those strange apple slices have become my favorite camping folklore. They're a little too weird to reproduce at home, but that morning they were just right.

Camping always sneaks up on you with some unexpected way to make you smile. Camping does the cliché stuff that feels good: it shakes the bolts loose and cleans out the cobwebs. You might find yourself thinking like an Iron Chef or channeling your eccentric home economics teacher. You might show off your derriere like a proud peacock over a piece of fruit. And you may ask yourself, how did I ever get by without camping?

Thanks for Sharing

It wouldn't be fair to talk about all these tasty dishes and not fess up with a few of my pet recipes. So here are ten favorites. Some are traditional, some are indulgent, some every camper should experience at least once, and others do the belly good. Many steps can be done ahead of time at home for better packing and easier prepping in the backcountry. But that doesn't mean you can't wing it on the trail if that's more your style. Look for ways to repackage bulky ingredients, don't forget to write the directions on a slip of paper or right on the ziplock bags, and feel free to devise your own methods for streamlining. Most can be prepared on the stove or campfire. Any of these recipes can be tailored to your taste buds. And even better, they're all easy, yummy meals that are sure to tempt the troops.

Bannock

Bannock is as beloved among campers as jerky. It's easy, quick, hot, and good. It's breakfast, lunch, dinner, and snack. It's camp comfort food. First noted in Scotland and also a Native American staple, it's a multicultural, antique recipe for simple unleavened biscuits. Bannock has inspired endless variations, impassioned arguments, competitions, and even classes. The standard mix can be prepared either at home or on the trail in a plastic bag. The amount given here should be enough for one or two people, but experts agree you can never have too much bannock. Increase the ingredients proportionately to please more mouths.

1 cup flour
1 teaspoon baking powder
$^1/_4$ teaspoon salt
Water
Oil

Combine the flour, baking powder, and salt: this is your mix. Just before you're ready to cook up your bannock, slowly add water to the mix. About $^1/_2$ cup of water works in this mix. Squeeze and knead the plastic bag as you go to check the consistency. Stop adding water once you have a firm, sticky dough. Wet and mushy is bad. Now the beauty of bannock (aside from the taste): prepare it any damn way you please. Bake hunks of dough in an oiled, covered pot, pan, or skillet. Drop spoonfuls into hot oil and fry. Wrap the dough around the end of a stick and toast it over the fire. You can even drop bits of it into boiling water to make dumplings. The bannock is done when it's golden brown. Create your signature style by adding powdered milk, grated cheeses, spices, oats, dried fruit, or vegetables. You can't go wrong with this simple recipe. I guarantee you won't be able to keep up with the hungry campers gobbling up your biscuits.

Cheesy Oatmeal Pepper Bowls

Cheesy Oatmeal Pepper Bowls are evidence of all the good that results when cheese and camping meet. Don't be fooled—this recipe might come across like an attempt to push the gourmet envelope, but it was just the result of a campsite cheese freak-out. Despite their lowbrow beginnings, these babies are something I whip out when I want to silence the skeptics of simple camp cuisine.

1 cup quick oats
1 vegetable bouillon cube (or any salty seasoning)
Pinches of onion powder, garlic powder,
    chili powder, and black pepper
$1/2$ small onion
3 garlic cloves
1 jalapeño pepper (substitute 1 dried chili
    for easier prepping)
Oil
$1^2/_3$ cups water
Nice chunk of cheddar or your favorite cheese
    (about $1/2$ a brick)
2 bell peppers
Salt and pepper
4 squares aluminum foil, pepper-fitted

At home, toss the oats, bouillon, onion powder, garlic powder, chili powder, and pepper into a ziplock bag. At camp, prepare a campfire and let it burn down to hot coals. Dice the onion, chop the garlic, and seed and mince the jalapeño. Heat about 1 tablespoon of oil in a pot over medium heat and add the onion, garlic, and jalapeño. Fry just until they begin to soften, then add the water. Bring to a boil. Add the oat mix, lower the heat, and simmer, stirring, until the mixture is thick like oatmeal. While the oatmeal cooks, cut 8 thin slices of the cheese and set aside; cube the rest. Once the oatmeal is done, add the cheese cubes and stir until they are melted and mixed. Cut the bell peppers in half lengthwise and remove the seeds. Rub with oil and sprinkle with salt and pepper. Place each half in the center of a foil square. Fill them with cheesy oatmeal and lay 2 cheese slices over the top of each. Fold up the aluminum foil sides to completely cover, but try to make a dome over the tops so the cheese doesn't stick to the foil. Bake in the campfire coals (or on a grate over the fire) for 8 to 10 minutes, until the peppers are soft. If you've got the space in your pack, a small can of salsa served over the top makes these tastier, and prettier too.

Chili-Lime Roasted Corn on the Cob

Chili-Lime Roasted Corn on the Cob feels and tastes like something you should eat outdoors. It's messy but refreshing. It also provides an easy down-home opportunity for genuine campfire cooking.

    Juice of 1 lime
    2 tablespoons oil
    1 teaspoon chili powder
    Salt and pepper
    2 ears of corn, husked
    2 squares aluminum foil, big enough to
       wrap corn in a well-sealed boat

Prepare a campfire and let it burn down to hot coals. Squeeze the lime juice into a ziplock bag and add the oil, chili powder, and a pinch of salt and pepper. Seal and shake the bag to thoroughly mix. Place one ear of corn on top of each aluminum foil square. Turn up the ends of the foil to make a boat for the juice drippings. Poke a hole in a corner of the bag and squeeze an equal amount of marinade out onto each ear, reserving a little marinade to squeeze on just before you eat. Rub to fully coat the ears and wrap them tightly in foil. Place in the campfire coals to roast for 8 to 10 minutes, turning occasionally to cook evenly. When you're ready to chow down, poke one end with a knife, fashion holders out of foil, or let them cool until you can touch them comfortably.

Fantasy Bananas

Fantasy Bananas were renamed on the GLOK trip. Banana Boat is their street name. When I first added bananas to our shopping list, the girls guffawed. "We don't have room for all these bananas!" "We don't need another dessert!" "We want s'mores!" But I brought them anyway, and they thanked me for it. Their warm, mushy sweetness won the hearts of all the GLOK, who vowed never to side with s'mores again. These will surpass your fantasy for a campfire dessert—hence the new and improved name.

> 2 unpeeled bananas
> 1 chocolate bar or a handful of chocolate chips
> 2 squares aluminum foil, banana-fitted

Prepare a campfire and let it burn down to hot coals. Slit the bananas with a knife lengthwise, cutting through the skin and halfway through the banana. Be careful to stop before you reach the ends. Break up the chocolate bar and slip an even number of squares or chips into the pocket in each banana. Wrap each banana up in a square of foil and place in the campfire coals (or even on a grate over the fire) for 4 to 5 minutes. Carefully open on a plate and eat the delicious mess with a spoon or fork.

Hot Sweet Whiskey Beans

Hot Sweet Whiskey Beans are a racy take on an ordinary dish. These lascivious legumes let your taste buds wax nostalgic without boring the heck out of them. They also provide a nutritional excuse to tote along whiskey (just in case you need one). I like to use 1 teaspoon chipotle and 1 teaspoon regular old cayenne hot sauce in this dish. And I prefer it sweet, but salty, so I always add an extra pinch of salt before digging in.

2 tablespoons brown sugar
2 teaspoons hot sauce
1 teaspoon barbecue sauce
5 dashes Worcestershire sauce
Salt and pepper
$1/2$ small onion
2 garlic cloves
1 can pink beans (pintos, great northerns,
   or kidneys work too)
Oil
Whiskey

At home, mix the sugar, hot sauce, barbecue sauce, Worcestershire, and hearty pinches of salt and pepper in a small ziplock bag. At camp, chop the onion and crush the garlic. Pour a little of the juice from the can of beans into the trash but keep the rest to thicken the sauce. Heat about 1 tablespoon of oil in a pot over medium heat. Add the onion and garlic, and cook until they begin to soften. Stir in the sauce mixture and cook for 1 minute. Be careful not to let it thicken too much just yet. Add the beans and cook for another minute or so. Now for the fun part—add the whiskey. Go once around the pot pouring lightly (about 1 tablespoon). Bring it to a boil, lower the heat, and let simmer for about 5 minutes. Give it a taste before serving to adjust for your salt and pepper preference.

Lentil Burgers

Lentil Burgers are the most complicated of my camp recipes, and they're still not complicated. I like them because they're a filling, trail-friendly meal that doesn't rely heavily on carbohydrates. And they satisfy an urge for a cookout classic—the burger. The only drawback is that you'll need to do some pretrip preparing with a food processor. Turn the mix into burgers and eat with cheese the old-fashioned way, or make balls and fry them up as fritters with rice or a vegetable. Experiment with different grains, beans, nuts, and spices (in the same proportions) to create a different-flavored patty.

$^1/_2$ cup red lentils
$^1/_2$ cup green lentils
$^1/_2$ cup quick oats
$^1/_2$ cup corn flakes
$^1/_4$ cup sunflower seeds
$^1/_4$ cup sesame seeds
3 tablespoons breadcrumbs
1 teaspoon onion powder
1 teaspoon garlic powder
1 teaspoon black pepper
Pinch of salt
Hot water
1 soy sauce packet
Oil

At home, grind the lentils in a food processor until they look like coarse sand. You can try grinding the red and green lentils separately for a finer grind or just throw them in all at once. Transfer the grounds to a big ziplock bag and add all the remaining ingredients except the water, soy sauce, and oil. You'll have about $2^1/_2$ cups of mix, enough to make 4 to 8 burgers or 40 to 50 fritters, depending on how big you like them. Bring the whole bag on your trip or divvy it up into individual servings—put 1 cup of mix in a small ziplock bag for 2 or 3 burgers or 16 to 20 fritters.

On the trail, carefully pour $1^1/_4$ cups hot water into the ziplock bag (use $^1/_2$ cup of hot water for 1 cup of mix). I rest the bag inside my soup pot for this part. Add the whole packet of soy sauce ($^1/_3$ of a packet for the 1 cup of mix). Once it's cool enough to touch, knead the ziplock bag to blend the mix. Let it sit and soften for about 20 minutes. Now, form patties or balls, and fry in a well-oiled skillet or pot over a medium flame. Cook until brown on both sides, about 5 minutes on each side. My favorite way to eat these is over lemony couscous, but sometimes I just nibble on them right out of the pan.

Peanut Butter Apple Tacos

Peanut Butter Apple Tacos are the perfect breakfast for easing sleepyheads out of their slumber, but they also double as lunch or a midnight snack. Sometimes I remember to snag an extra packet of honey from my favorite tea shop especially for these, and I'm always happy I did. One small suggestion—when you eat these, have a cup of water, tea, or coffee handy, or you'll have to contend with a serious case of cement mouth.

6 tablespoons peanut butter (chunky gets my vote)
2 flour tortillas
1 apple (Red Delicious, Fuji, Pink Lady—your choice)
Oil

It's a messy job, but start at home by putting the peanut butter into a ziplock bag. At camp, slather about 3 tablespoons of peanut butter on each tortilla. Slice the apple into 12 to 16 thin slices. (You'll have some apple left over for munching while these cook.) Layer half the slices on one half of each tortilla. If you brought the honey, pour some on each and fold the tortillas in half over the apple filling. Heat about $1/2$ tablespoon of oil in any pot, pan, or skillet over medium heat. Fry each taco for 2 to 3 minutes on each side, until both sides are golden brown.

Savory S'mores

Savory S'mores are less a recipe than a rebellion. Why should marshmallow lovers get to have all the old-school campfire fun? Members of the Marshmallow Haters' Club can still hold things on sticks over the campfire and make a big gooey mess. Quantities aren't very important in this recipe—just keep making as many as your belly can handle.

Roasting sticks
Cheese cubes (a firm, springy cheese
   like Swiss or Muenster is a must)
Chocolate bar
Square crackers (your favorite)

First, seek out the prefect roasting stick—long, thin, and green (or live). Whittle the end to make the perfect Mr. Pointy or just use as is. Cube a few pieces of cheese and spear them through the center. Break off a square of chocolate and place it on a cracker. Now, hold your cheese over the tips of the flames until it's nice and melted. Be careful—cheese doesn't have the synthetic stickiness of marshmallows, so overcooking can lead to lost cheese. Hold the chocolate-and-cracker layer under the cooked cheese cube and hold another cracker over the top. Squeeze and pull the cheese off the end of the stick. In one swoop you'll create a sandwich and warm the chocolate up to mingle with the cheese. The only thing left to do now is shove the whole thing into your mouth. Taking a dainty bite is only looking for trouble.

Tipsy Peaches

Tipsy Peaches are yet another intoxicating camp dish. Like Fantasy Bananas, they are a fanciful campfire dessert, but unlike those sweet treats, these are sexy as hell. Experiment with any fruit and spirits you have at camp. I've discovered that pears love red wine and apples prefer whiskey.

1 peach
2 squares aluminum foil, big enough
    to fashion peachy purses
2 tablespoons brown sugar
4 tablespoons whiskey or red wine

Prepare a campfire and let it burn down to hot coals. Halve and pit the peach. Place one half in the center of each aluminum foil square and fold up the sides to catch the liquid. Rub each peach half with a tablespoon of sugar to roughly coat. Pour 2 tablespoons of whiskey or wine into each foil cup, just enough to make a small, low pool for the peach half. Pull the foil up around the sides and seal at the top, like a little purse. Place in the campfire coals (or on a grate) and let stew for 5 to 7 minutes, until the peach looks and feels soft and the edges are brown and translucent. Open carefully and eat with a spoon or fork. Then pour the delicious juice into a cup for sipping.

Trail Rice

Trail Rice is a little bit Indian, a little bit lumberjack. It was inspired in part by the delicately spiced rice, raisin, and cashew Indian dishes I am so addicted to, and in part by nagging culinary curiosity. Every camping trip, I kept coming back to the same question, "What happens if you fry trail mix?" Duh! Of course tastiness happens every time you throw fruit and nuts into oil with spices. A mix with chocolate or peanut butter chips might not work in this recipe, but any fruit and nut combination rocks. Go wild—my favorite includes papaya, cranberries, banana chips, cashews, peanuts, and almonds.

Oil
1 cup fruit and nut trail mix
1 cup basmati rice
1 teaspoon garam masala
   (use more for a spicier version)

Salt and pepper
1 ¹/₂ cups water

Heat about 1 tablespoon oil in pot over a medium high flame. Add the trail mix and toast for 2 to 3 minutes, until very fragrant, being careful not to burn it. Add the dry rice, garam masala, and a pinch of salt and pepper. Stir to mix, and fry for another minute or so. Add the water and bring to a boil. Lower the heat. Cover and simmer for 20 minutes, or until the rice is cooked and water is absorbed. Add more salt and pepper to taste.

White Lightning, Bug Juice, Mountain Dew— Stalking the Wild Liquids

I recently had an alarming realization: I was almost never comfortable from the ages of about eighteen to twenty-one years old. I teetered all over Boston in knee-high boots, baby doll dresses, and skin-tight T-shirts. I had a pathetic, die-hard loyalty to fashion before function. Practicality is still not my strong suit. I will sacrifice logic for caprice in certain situations. This is one of them. I camp with wine. I don't pour it into plastic or use cardboard picnic boxes; I mean glass bottles of wine. And not once have I ever cursed my frivolity or regretted the backache. Nothing screams bacchanal like wine beside a campfire in the middle of nowhere. So I bring it, every time. After I get the tent up, it's time to uncork the Cabernet and toast to another successful pitching. Feel more sporty? Crack open a few cold ones instead. A six-pack will stay cool enough without ice to get you through the first night. After that something with more punch is needed for the rest of the trip. Enter the tequila or whiskey. A little goes a long way, and it's surprisingly palatable from plastic. The GLOK turned up their noses at cactus juice and sought southern comfort in a bottle of bourbon. It certainly provides a toastiness that goes nicely with a campfire. Whichever hard stuff you prefer, dispense it into a disposable plastic, or go for classic with a flask.

There's plenty of time and ample space for cosmic wandering, but camping can be a naughty, raucous, even raunchy affair without the help of chemicals. The naked world is stimulating all by itself. Escape to Camp Cleanse—gorge yourself on water and roughage, and come home a shiny new woman. If you do fancy a swig, a swill, or a swallow, be careful. You're in unfamiliar territory, so keep your wits about you, tend to the fire, and prepare your bear precautions. Get a good lay of the land. Keep a flashlight nearby so there's no unnecessary stumbling, and keep drinking that water.

I thought I should exercise discretion and forgo my wine habit for the sake of the GLOK, but they wouldn't have it. When I tried to caution against three bottles, they emailed, "Give me wine, or give me death." Commitment to hedonism isn't as easy as it looks. On the trail, we had to quash a minor uprising from Rachel, who kept muttering something about plastic jugs under her breath. And Jen, daughter of a sommelier, claimed she was scandalized at drinking Pinot Noir out of a metal cup. Don't forget, ladies, camping is sacrifice. ❧

Welcome-Back Wings

Intoxicated clinking of cups or not, your camping feasts will be as luscious as a busty Renaissance Festival. They'll be comforting like Mom's tomato soup on a rainy day. Nourishing like a sprout sandwich on whole grain toast from a vegan hole-in-the-wall. Madcap like midnight schemes involving pickles, cream cheese, sauerkraut, and peanut butter. Delicious, decadent, damn good—all the naughty *d* words. Your camp fare can be just about anything you dream up, but it won't be deep-fried and served up by a cute waiter in tight jeans. There won't be eggs over easy, spider rolls, anchovy pizza, or chicken tikka masala. There won't be a list of piping-hot greasy appetizers or a kick-ass selection of cold imported beer. These bits of heaven are reserved for the Postcamping-Trip Eating Extravaganza (PCTEE).

The PCTEE is an important camping tradition. It's a reintegration ritual with a buffet. As soon as the trip is over, your motley crew will trudge into a nearby restaurant and chow down on all the stuff camping doesn't allow. You won't be wearing makeup and your hair will look like crap. Civilized women will sneak glances at you in the bathroom mirror. Some customers will suspect you broke out of prison and put on clothes dug out of a dumpster. But you won't care. There will be no shortage of memories and victories to celebrate. You'll order way more food than you can handle and maybe a few stiff drinks. Hysterics will ensue. Spitting might occur. Food pieces could shoot out of a nostril. Waxing philosophical is completely unavoidable.

Picking the right barrelhouse to grace with your ripe presence is key. Online forums are filled with reviews of popular camper haunts. Check out the pizza place where all the climbers hang, or christen your own stomping ground. Wherever you end up, it won't be far from the forest or park parking lot. The promise of this meal guarantees you won't be able to hold out very long. I usually either put my faith in a local dive with an inappropriate name or embark on a wild goose chase to fulfill a peculiar craving. It's hard to disappoint a feral girl, but choose wisely.

Hungry, cranky, and just a little sick of each other, we GLOK exercised poor communication skills and a complete lack of patience when choosing the location for our debauchery. Proper rip-roaring revelry cannot be had in a huge commercial chain hawking mediocre food. Even the so-called "ecstasy fries" couldn't bring about joy at our table. Confusion over how many buffalo wings were ordered opened the floodgates of verbal jousting. Laura busted out with a controversial remark aimed at me: "You only like camping because of the postcamping food." No one said much after that, and I tortured myself through the rest of my crappy wings. *It's my hips, isn't it?* I thought, before moving on to *I eat like a barbarian* and then *Shit, I'm a terrible camper.* Back on the road, one pit stop and a tight squeeze later, the hatchets were buried.

At home, I turned to my camping journal to think about what she'd said. My entry starts: "Laura is right. Almost." Of course the postcamping meal isn't the only reason I like camping. I wouldn't go through all this just for a get-out-of-jail-and-eat-as-much-bad-food-as-you-want card. I do love it though. Maybe as much as the actual camping. It's hard-earned, well-deserved, unabashed abundance. It's like spending a day in a dark room and finally turning on the lights. I savor every bit of my jalapeño quesadillas with ranch sour cream. I appreciate the orange light from the dim lamp above my table. I notice my waitress's neat handwriting and the flowery soap in the bathroom. I even smile at loud bratty kids. A clean, flushing toilet has the power to make me giddy. That's exciting for folks who ordinarily live in a place where almost anything can be had at any time. When you first enter the warm, delicious air of the restaurant, it's like walking on your shaky fawn legs again. Camping makes that wild rebirth possible. Without camping it would just be another day in fried paradise.

🐾 🐾 🐾 🐾 🐾

Tipsy peaches, cheese galore, well-earned fried food—you must be a camping convert by now. If not, maybe there's one question still haunting you. It's the question all noncampers, especially the ones accustomed to twenty-four-hour everything, ask. What do you do out there?

Build a fire. Sing a song. Cartwheel. Stargaze. Make out. Swim. Scream. Hike. Draw. Knit. Or just sit. Chapter 6 will quell all your fears about backcountry boredom.

Chill Like a Sloth, Flit Like a Hummingbird

What is there to do out there?

The uninitiated all ask the same question, "What do you do out there?" They put an emphasis on the second *do*, usually to imply one of three things. The cool kids say it with a sneer, suggesting anything outside the city limits is either drudgery or just plain dull. My camping-virgin comrades say it with wide eyes and a slight shiver, as if the forest is creeping and crawling all over them. And my prolific Italian relatives say it with a wink, insinuating the only reason anyone camps is to get some hot, sweaty animal sex. They're all a little right. There is work to be done. There are some disarming critters. And the wild does inspire especially good sex. But they're a little wrong too. Time out there is never boring or tiresome. The minor hardships (black crickets, achy legs, greasy hair) are always worth enduring. And though the great outdoors might make you horny, you'll also be tempted to cartwheel, shimmy, ponder, yodel, sniff, and leap. The city is dreamy—late-night tacos and movies, skateboarders with Mohawks, flea markets, smart graffiti, deliveries of any item with just a phone call—but I have never once paced around my campsite lamenting the lack of good Thai or dreaming about how I could be lying on the couch watching music videos. In the backcountry you won't feel you've been snatched away from civilization; you will feel as though you narrowly escaped its clutches.

Mornings that aren't kicked off by beeping, ringing, buzzing, and thumping set the tone for a different kind of day. Cool, misty daybreak asks "What would you like to explore today, my primitive princess?" No demands, no errands, no interruptions, and nothing to buy. No bathroom rituals or morning talk shows. It's culture shock. At first you may be disoriented, but then caffeine deprivation strikes, and you'll set about boiling water. In the backcountry, fulfilling basic needs is not as easy as opening the fridge or as instant as hitting a switch. Autopilot is decidedly off. Camp life demands active participation and Zen-like deliberation, but there's no need for chore charts. Remember how fun it was to build a fort and play house? It's like that, but better. Now you get to play with matches, drink booze, and make out

Does this tree get reception? The only time I ever used my cell phone in the wild was to call my mom. It was my first time successfully climbing a tree in eleven years, and I wanted the lady who kissed my childhood scrapes to be the first to know. Two things camping will surely do for you: revive your tree-climbing skills and give you bragging rights. ❧

for real, and no one calls you to come in and take a bath. Even if your apartment is mayhem, you just might skip around organizing camp. You might volunteer to make breakfast, even if you normally snag a last-minute bagel. Routines and habits are shot to hell. Modernity and its responsibilities melt away. Natural occurrences like sunrise and sunset dictate the schedule, and the day takes on an easy, comfortable rhythm.

We woke on Saturday morning to two forlorn campers hovering around the GLOK site. The only decent place for their tent was awkwardly close to our private oasis. They bashfully joked about their wives letting them out once a year, and they slowly eased into being our neighbors. As we took off for a long hike, they were setting up two chairs conspicuously pointed away from our camp. When we returned they were waving and yelling, "You missed it!" "Missed what, neighbor?" Laura asked. "That," they said through huge, goofy grins and pointed to a thirty-foot tree branch on the ground. There they'd been sitting, minding their own business, when the heavy limb had come tumbling out of the sky and crashed down in the clearing between our sites. "Wow," we all replied in unison. They nodded. We looked at the branch with renewed interest. We took pictures of it and bent our necks back to study the massive tree that had let it go. Four city gals, who've collectively seen enough car accidents and bar brawls to fill a Bruce Willis movie, were completely taken in by the mystery of a big fallen stick. Camping alters the perspective of the most sophisticated slickers, and simplicity becomes the day's entertainment. 🐾

Stoked to Stoke

Camp life is pleasantly paced with fulfilling, enjoyable tasks. Once you've pitched the tent, arranged your space, sipped the wine, and taken in your kingdom, next up is building a fire. The campfire is the heart of camp, the common room where lots of hanging happens. Fire building requires time, effort, and patience, but every bit of it is fun. Campers clamor over who will be the keeper of the flame, especially the ladies. Pyromania is rarely encouraged in little girls. Now we get to mess around with wood, wield a big stick, and watch proudly as the bright chemical reaction we built warms the faces of our friends.

Head over to the fire pit—the sooty spot surrounded by a ring of rocks. Look around. Don't build a fire near bushes that might catch fire and boulders that might be scarred by flames and smoke. Look up. Steer clear of low-hanging branches that could spark a major fire when heat and embers rise. Look down. A stable circle of rocks should surround the pit. If not, rebuild. The rock ring is essential for preventing the fire from spreading, and it adds a homey touch. Rocks abound—carry or roll them over. They should be about the size of a high-top sneaker and arranged to touch. While you're at it, grab a few flat ones for resting drinks and preparing meals. But be careful, and kind— you could be overturning a creature's summer cottage.

While you're working on the hearth, send out the troops to gather wood. Gathering is a team effort. Wood may be scarce or wet, and sometimes the sad reality is you just can't get enough.

That's no excuse to yank or cut anything off living trees—ouch! All your firewood should be found on the ground. Split up, and cover a wide area so you don't strip one part of the forest bare. Look for dry wood on high ground. If it's rained recently, check under bushes and leaves for drier stashes. Aim for three rough sizes: pretzel-thin twigs, pepperoni-width branches, and bigger, pork roast–like logs. Try snapping the twigs and branches. If they break cleanly, they're dry. If they bend and twist, they're probably too fresh, or live. Logs are too thick to test this way, but live wood is often heavier than dried. Live logs also retain a youthful, unblemished bark. Leave any logs longer than two feet—they just won't fit in the pit. And be wary of pine—it gives off a lot of smoke and sparks. Dry-rotted wood is decayed through and ultralight. It makes decent *tinder*—the dry, light material used to spark a fire—because it burns up fairly quickly. Paper and cardboard from camp are ideal tinder, but dried leaves, bark, and grasses are what castaways use.

No means *no*. If fires are prohibited, don't even consider breaking the rules to build your campfire. Even if fires are permitted, be cautious in extremely windy or dry conditions, and always build in an established pit. In the desert or at the beach wood is at times impossible to find, and fires are often restricted. If circumstances aren't right, relocate or ditch the fire all together. Toss a few candles into your pack for this occasion. Not as exciting as a campfire, but they do provide a cozy glow. ❦

Many factors—size of the pit, type of wood, duration of the fire—affect how much wood a fire needs. You'll develop a feel for how much to gather. A few armfuls should be enough to start. Back at camp, designate a spot a few feet from the fire pit for the woodpile. If rain is predicted, stash it under a lean-to or tuck it under a tarp. Break up twigs and branches. You'll need varying lengths (all under two feet), but be sure to reserve one long, sturdy branch for the fire keeper—getting to poke at the fire is one of the rewards for building it. Snap stubborn sticks in half by picking one end up off the ground and stomping in the center with the opposite foot. Get a better grip by slipping on cloth work gloves. Ask the person with the neatest sock drawer to separate the heap into three smaller piles by girth. Once the wood is sorted, the magic starts.

My first fire fizzled, and so did my second and third. But determined, and gifted with a patient cohort, I tore down and rebuilt my fire three times before it finally caught. Starting from scratch at least once is inevitable, unless you're a creepy nine-year-old Drew Barrymore. Everyone—even you—will be antsy for the fireworks to begin, but rushing through the early construction phase will likely lead to failure. Fire building is an

Gathering wood can be addictive. You get this frenzied feeling you can't give up because you just might happen upon the mother lode. Sound familiar? Kind of like scouring thrift stores for the ultimate salt and pepper shakers (my favorite to date: a tie between sad turnips and nesting lightning bolts). ❧

exercise in delayed gratification. And like many camping procedures, there are countless sworn-by systems. I'm sure they're all great. I know one classic way that works just about every time, to hell with variety. The teepee method is aptly named because, duh, the wood is piled in the shape of a teepee. The two teepee qualities to shoot for are sturdy and loose. If it's not sturdy, it could collapse and snuff out your baby embers. And if it's not loose, oxygen won't flow through the sticks and feed the fire.

First, make a crumpled pile of tinder in the center of the pit. Now take four or five pepperoni branches. Stand them up, leaning against each other over the tinder pile, to form the frame of your teepee. The tip of the teepee should be one to two feet off the ground. Grab the top where they meet and shake. Is your teepee sturdy? If it isn't, this is a good time to start over. Work your way around the teepee, laying on more branches and twigs, until you have what looks like a shoddy, cone-shaped basket. Make sure there are lots of holes everywhere for thin twigs—*kindling*—and tinder. Go around again and poke the thinnest twigs into your teepee, parallel with the

Is your camping trip a birthday celebration? Commemorate it with birthday candles stuck into your bannock (check out the recipe for this classic camp carbohydratey goodness in chapter 5). Leftover candles are excellent tinder. Those trick candles that never blow out are particularly good for tormenting birthday girls *and* getting the fire started. 🐾

ground. Then shove a few more wads of tinder through the remaining holes.

Now for the moment—or more likely, moments—of truth. Your teepee is sturdy and littered with flammables. There are plenty of pockets for airflow. But there are still no guarantees. Did you kneel before the sequoias of fires past? Did you put an orange-peel offering in your sleeping bag? Hold a flame up to a bit of paper or tinder peeking out of your teepee. Walk around the teepee and light up a few more exposed spots. Chant. Cross your fingers. As the wads burn up, ideally they'll take some of the twigs with them. And if enough smaller sticks burn, they'll ignite the bigger branches. Sometimes the stuff just burns out too quickly to catch anything substantial. Don't worry, it's simply time to fiddle. Picture a bunch of mechanics standing around a smoking car. It takes a little bit of guesswork, a fraction of science, a pinch of magic, and a speck of luck. You'll develop your own bag of tricks for getting out of fire purgatory. Here's a few that I play with: grab the top and shake the teepee gently to encourage the airflow and awaken embers. Stuff more paper in where things haven't caught, then light them. Focus on the base of the teepee. Poke the teepee with a few more well-placed twigs. Fan the embers with a plastic plate. Shake, light, poke, and fan some more. When it catches, you'll know. You'll have an impulse to step back and watch in awe as it grows.

Once your teepee is completely up in flames, add a few more pepperoni branches to the frame. Reserve the twigs and tinder for starting over tomorrow. Poke with your fire-keeper stick. Rein in errant embers and branches. Eventually your teepee will collapse. Now you can add big branches or logs; this slow-burning stuff is called *fuel*. Two pork roast–like pieces at one time are usually enough. Crisscross them so air can flow under and between. Sit, stare, and relax. Cook and be cozy. And when it's time to turn in, make sure everything has burned up to a fine white ash. Pour water into the pit and stir. Add more water and keep stirring. Don't stop until you can rest easy the fire is completely out. Congratulations are in order—doesn't it feel good to be keeper of the flame?

Verb, Verb, Verb Your Noun

Some say a fire isn't a campfire without s'mores, but those over-rated hoof sandwiches are the biggest disappointment of my camping experience. I say a campfire isn't a campfire without a sing-along. Don't balk. Even my most tight-lipped buddies can't resist carrying a tune around the fire. Nonchalantly hum just one line of "California Dreamin'" and wait for the seed to grow. Pick something everyone knows. Or go prepared—from ancient chants to childish ditties, any lyrics can be dug up on the web. Make enough copies to go around. Remove key words and mad lib the blanks. Now Liza's hole isn't in the bucket, it's in her muffler, and you're not row, row, rowing your boat, you're pour, pour, pouring shots up and down the bar. Too shy to belt it out? The same trick can be pulled on old ghost stories. Or spin an original group yarn—work around the circle, each person adding one sentence. Flashlights in mouths, shadow puppets, and rustling leaves add instant drama. End the night with a group squeeze. Borrow this precious tradition from those sweet Girl Scouts. As the last embers burn, everyone joins hands. In turn, each person makes a private wish and squeezes the hand of the next person, who then does the same, until the wave makes it back around. Too sugarcoated for you? Spice it up by requiring secret wishes be traded for juicy public confessions—this way, the night might never end.

What about flameless evenings? Some campers abstain from fires altogether, but they still camp happily. Throw a tarp on the ground. Spread a blanket or sleeping bag over it. Lie back and look up. City light and smog block out the night sky. I never saw a shooting star until I started camping. Now I can't keep count of the ones I've followed—huge glowing hunks of green and baby blue starlets in tandem. Stargazing is just as romantic as it looks in the movies, but it's not reserved for

'Fraid of the dark? There's still plenty of party to be had inside. Rig a flashlight from above (or stick it in your gear loft), and your tent will light up like a lantern. Host poker, thumb wrestle, read, or lie back and listen. What are you hearing? Critters rustling and hustling to get safely home. Professions of love and desperate cries for a quickie. There's the familiar creepy cardboard sound grasshoppers and crickets make as they rub parts of their bodies together. And howling coyotes summon each other across miles to schedule their reunions. There's an owl with a hoot strangely reminiscent of "who cooks for you?" Flying squirrels' chirps are often mistaken for birds'. But my favorite night call is the blunt honk of bullfrogs arguing over mating rights. So romantic. ❦

couples. Platonic pals make great astronomers too. Pass the bottle. Test your knowledge. Take notes. Chart Orion's Belt, the Dippers, and your astrological signs. Or connect your own dots. I discovered the Juicy Hamburger in New Hampshire with my cousin Danielle and the Tiny Tambourine in Ohio with my main squeeze. And sky gazing isn't just for night folk. Don't forget to stop and watch the clouds too. Where you saw a turtle as a child, you might discover Michael Jackson today.

Light My (Other) Fire

Camping may be the naughtiest vacation ever. The sun makes for moist, bare bodies. Lungs are full with fresh invigorating air. Active muscles are taut and ready for action. Nature calls. Frisky squirrels wrestle and rile up their hormones, while bees play pimp to budding flowers. Everywhere you turn is the set of a porno flick—the too-small tent, a field of tall grass, a waterfall flowing into a natural whirlpool. There's plenty of wind to throw caution to, and no one is watching. Let your inner exhibitionist come out and play. Sparrows may snicker, but they won't call the police. Sex in the great outdoors is the

Have a camper who won't buck up? Maybe the forest fornicators are too much to compete with. Invite your pal to build a love nest in the tent. Who can resist a private game of truth or dare? Have any of us really outgrown our teenage fantasies of being the zit-free make-out maven? Close quarters are hot. And provisional close quarters are even hotter. 🐾

essence of lusty frivolity. Maybe disaster scenarios do it for me, but the feeling that you're the last two people left on the planet conjures serious urges. And don't fear that your not wearing lipstick or having perfect hair will put a damper on your drive. You're a sweaty, messy, wild disaster, and that's pretty damn empowering, not to mention sexy. Scream. Yelp. Howl. Screw inhibition.

There are the occasional obvious hazards of a rock in the back and sand-scraped knees. Clear away twigs and pebbles. Seek out a bed of soft moss. Lay a blanket by the fire. Sit on a towel instead of a bare boulder. The sex can be barbaric, but the pain doesn't have to be. Mist bug spray so mosquitoes don't take advantage of uncovered parts. Shake out your clothes before you dress. Turn the postcoital tick check into foreplay for another go around. The hardest thing about camping sex isn't the floor, it's staying fresh as a flower. Keep a stash of baby wipes handy. Sponge off with warm water and powder your puff. Don't underestimate the backcountry's abilities to inspire, provoke, suggest, and expose. Pack extra protection. A camping trip is a jaunt back to the basics. What could be more basic than our animal instincts? Find a safe place to stash your camping journal back at home—it is sure to be X-rated.

PG-13 Possibilities

Camp should be bustling with the activity of ladies (and gents) following their most neglected fancies. The whole gang—craftress, party girl, tomboy, layabout, and geek—can have those special cravings fulfilled on a trip to the backcountry. Witness your friends at their bravest (and their silliest). Test your own courage. Work on those cartwheels. Beat your old jump-rope record. Study tiny life through a magnifying glass. Can't dance? Who cares? Check in—there's never enough time in the real world to sit and talk. Or check out—waste away the afternoon dreaming. The middle of nowhere is the precise location for perfecting potentially embarrassing new tricks, pursuing wild whims, and resurrecting old-school favorites.

Get Girly

Most urban gals raised by apartment-hopping families never have the opportunity to pitch a tent in lush, suburban backyard grass like the kids do in credit card commercials. Let's set our slumber parties loose on the wild. Invite your best girlfriends and play Mansion-Apartment-Shack-House next to a stream. Spill your guiltiest celebrity crushes around the fire. Need pranks to fulfill your sleepover fantasy? Treat the girls

The sound of silence. Now that the iPod people have taken over, it's harder to make the case against bringing along tunes. But purists and your primitive neighbors would agree: leave the electronics home. Try a trip without, if only to prove you can break the habit. Play an infectiously appropriate song in the parking lot just before you hike in. A few choice Buck 65 and Madonna tracks carried the GLOK all through the weekend. Still need a fix? Teach yourself harmonica. 🐾

to a spruce adorned with their demi-cup push-ups. Separate the B.F.'s from the G.F.'s with trust falls: pair off and take turns falling backward. Or huddle up behind a boulder and have one person drop, while you all play catch. The thrill of falling and the release of letting go are a lot more fun without the dread of gym class.

Get Creative

Read short plays. Act out skits. Your troop's rendition of *Equus* will have the locals lining up around the tree stump. *The Pigman*, my teenage obsession, is penned in the voice of a mischievous boy and his demure girlfriend. My fella and I spent a tent-bound weekend passing the book and reading aloud. You don't have to be an actor; in fact, it's more fun if you're not. More a visual type? Hand out disposable cameras and hold photo shoots with ferns. Nature shots are great postcards and look impressive framed back at home. Or try the ultimate found-object art: Stone People. Each camper hunts down her own big rock and creates a person where it lies. Build upward or outward—pebbles as eyes, twigs as arms, dirt for hair. Then

A pile of serious reading grows on my nightstand. I flog myself regularly for not getting to it all, but I still don't bring those books camping. Offbeat selections that might not take priority at home—childhood favorites and hokey horrors—go on vacation instead. Without this policy I might never have rediscovered how *Harriet the Spy* made me cry, or why *The Thief of Always* was worth being an hour late to my eighth-grade dance. ❧

hold a showing. Serve wine and cheese. The best part is searching the forest for the hidden denizens.

Get Competitive

Got the gambling bug? The GLOK stayed up all night, occupied with six dice, whiskey, and gossip. Dice and cards are lightweight and pocket-sized and make for endless games. Or bring four golf balls and play a bastard version of bocce. Throw out one (the *jack*), and give everyone a chance to come closest

---

Those damn Scouts! Every time I hear about the stuff they do, I curse myself for being a pasty kid who preferred libraries and movie theaters. (The Scout website, conveniently linked for you in the resources section, is a great source for all Scout stuff.)

- What Fell? A game for the dark when all is quiet. One person stands outside the tent and drops something, while everyone else uses their senses to guess what it was. Was it a leaf or a headband? A twig or a lighter? A leg warmer or a tube sock?

- Shazam! Any weird word will do. Every time someone says it, all campers must stop what they're doing and dance for fifteen seconds. Anyone abusing the magic word must dance for a full minute, naked. (I added that part. Scouts don't play like that.)

- Nature's Cacophony. Everyone gets a few minutes to find two things that make noise when hit together. Then it's time for band practice. If you're lucky, the birds will provide backup. ❧

with the other three balls. Whoever wins gets to throw out the jack next. Want something more cutthroat? How about a game of war? Water guns are easy to pack and make for a devilish summer frolic. Surprise camp with a sudden onslaught, or play it fair and arm your enemies first.

And Get a Move On

I was on a week-long ladies-only trip during a steamy South Carolina summer. At night we tossed and turned as if we had fevers. When we woke it was already too hot to find respite in coffee. Draped over logs and laid out right on the dirt, we were nine immobile, sweaty, grouchy bitches.

One afternoon the crankiest of our crew, Marisa, surprised us by suggesting a hike to a lake. No one had heard of any lake. No one really wanted to move. But no one wanted to

Competitive Comics is a game I invented in honor of the rain, and it's become one of my standards even on sunny days. Don't be fooled—this game isn't for people who can draw (I should know). It's about stretching your imagination, not artistic talent. Each person gets a piece of paper and her favorite writing instrument. Form teams of two partners. Then draw boxes (or circles, octagons—whatever) in any arrangement, to fill up the page, just like a comic strip. Next, give your strip a title. Anything's fair game: "Mr. Wiggly Attends a Picnic," "Yellow," "Rhinoceros." No peeking. Pass your paper to your partner, who does the same. Now fill in the supplied boxes to tell the story of the title given. Take turns sharing your progress box by box, or disappear for hours to complete your masterpiece. ❧

let Marisa down, or hear her whine, so we heaved our bodies up and headed out. Five minutes into the trail, I was dripping. There was lots of excited talk about how awesome it would be to go swimming. Half an hour later, we were still just talking about it. "How much longer?" "Are we going the right way?" "Let me sit down for one stupid second," were common refrains. Marisa got dodgy and a few of us grew suspicious of her ability to locate the secret lake. Worse, a few others grew suspicious of the existence of the secret lake. An hour on the same path with no sign of it; it looked like there was a liar in our midst. A witch trial was unavoidable—everyone got and gave more than their share right there on the trail. Just when it seemed the cat fight might stop, an eerie cool breeze swept through, and within seconds we were drenched. Marisa laughed demonically as if she had planned it, and we turned back like a soggy, dejected pack of formerly wild alley cats. The sloping trail we had made our way in on was now a sloppy mudslide. In the first few minutes, two went down. There were stifled snickers. Then there was jumping and pushing. By the time we made it back everyone had rolled around in the muck at least once. We marched into camp muddy and rambunctious, like a bunch of victorious mud wrestlers. There was even some uncharacteristic high-fiving. We were still sweaty. And now we were dirty. Camp was a soaking wet mess. But crankiness couldn't touch us. We roared like accomplished mountain women, and we scoffed at heat and rain. The moral of this story: take a hike.

When I was a kid I'd let my grandmother drag me along the streets of Brooklyn to bakeries, butchers, and even smelly fish markets as long as she didn't mind hearing about my ach-

Hiking haiku. Because some advice is better in seventeen syllables. Compose your own back at camp in celebration of your treks—remember, arrange the syllables five-seven-five. Suggest group haiku time. They're traditionally tributes to nature, and they look adorable silk-screened on T-shirts and backpacks. I ironed this one onto a tank top:

Shape-shifting is real.
Tame purring kitty home, turns
tomcat on the trail.

Clunky boots won't do.
Feet prefer to know the ground
they meet underneath.

Fancy hiking boots aren't a necessity even on a hike. A trail shoe or sneaker with good ankle support will do the job too.

Swift or slow, you choose.
The turtle and hare both say,
screw the race today.

Walk at a comfortable pace and take breaks when you need them. And unless you're looking to haul ass, a four-hour hike is probably enough for one day.

No little girl lost.
Follow blazes of color,
or leave your own crumbs.

ing feet the whole time. Imagine a seven-year-old with aching feet. I grew to appreciate walking as a useful mode of transportation, but it was a long time before I accepted walks as

Every trail uses a system for marking. Look for *blazes*—paint splotches, reflectors, or metal signs on trees and rocks. Some forests and parks use freestanding poles with trail numbers on them. If you have a tendency to get lost, leave a marker with rope or cloth, or build a *cairn*—a distinguishable pile of rocks.

A prima donna.
She lugged her trunk and her junk,
alone, up the trail.

Bring plenty of water but don't bring plenty of other stuff to weigh you down.

Knee socks with shorts—hot!
Consider when choosing wear,
ticks, ivy, and thorns.

Even if it's warm, wear knee socks or pants. If you rub up against poison ivy you'll be protected, and there will be less skin exposed for a tick to hitch a ride. Tuck pants into socks for added protection, and avoid walking through brush and tall grass.

A spooky full moon,
beckons night owls with glimmer.
Turn off your flashlight!

Night hikes are tempting, especially when there's a full moon in a clear sky. You probably won't even need a flashlight if you take it slow. Turn it off, and for dark fun, whisper in a frantic voice "Did you hear that?" 🐾

leisure. Complaining is one of my talents, but it rarely inter-feres with my love for a good hike. Uphill, downhill, crossing streams, or through ravines—hiking rules. I've stumbled upon flocks of preening naked gay men, played hide and seek with a porcupine, followed a path of mushrooms that looked like spaceships, and dunked my head in gushing falls. Explore the territory. Trek to a vista. Walk until you're hungry, then plop down for a picnic. Seek out a shrouded nook for an afternoon tryst. Hiking is an obvious backcountry activity and one you don't want to miss. Plan a long hike for a day when you'll wake at camp and sleep there too. Prepare a snack. Sling the can-teen over your shoulder. Pick a path, and off you go. Use your guidebook, or wander at will. Either way, stick to the trails. Guidebooks and trail maps will suggest interesting destina-tions and give an estimate of how long trails might take. Leave

Get wet. Somewhere in between how often I think about food and how often I think about my hair is the frequency with which I dream about gliding through a natural pool of water (in my brown bikini and with flawless thighs). Particularly wonderful are swimming holes—secret, clear, and enchanting—but lakes, ponds, streams, and of course oceans, all rock my world. Brown tinted water is nothing to fear—it's just tannins from trees stain-ing the water, kind of like tea. Flip-flops and swift paddling make sure I don't accidentally brush up against anything yucky. Still too squeamish for the unfiltered, untreated fluid? Baptize your toes on a sultry day. Before you know it, you won't be able to resist doing the backstroke in the buff. ✿

ample time to make it back before dark. You'll want to rest, then have a predinner snack and possibly an aperitif before you embark on the evening's chores.

License to Chill

Seeking primitive pleasure is a cinch, but avoiding the back-country blues is even easier. The best advice: go with the flow. My biggest camping downers are bugs. Black crickets freaked me out in North Carolina; furry spiders chased the GLOK into our tent early; and sand fleas made me spaz out all over Fire Island. Rural bugs are weirder than their urban cousins. I know I'm not alone in my fear of them. Just move the party to your fabulously bug-free tent. We're not out there to conquer the forest or compete for Miss Fearless or prove our durability. Embrace what comes, come what may. Camping is a chance to kick off those precious but uncomfortable shoes. Loosen your grip. It really stinks when you forget the stove, but it stinks a lot less if you take it as an invitation to eat M&Ms with cheddar cheese on rye. Compromise. Confront your small dilemmas with spontaneity. When you're camping, the golden rule is "Be prepared, but then, just be flexible."

And don't skip out on camping just because some of this stuff reeks a bit too much of organized playtime. Is putting the kettle on to boil while you whittle a walking stick too bucolic for your taste? Think of the great outdoors as a new venue for any of your usual hobbies. Why should we be confined to dingy bars, crowded streets, and cramped apartments? Spread out.

The backcountry doesn't have to be reserved for folk who always get their full eight hours. Let's show the birds and the bees that humans weren't born wearing khaki cargo pants. Get out there and talk technology. Sit around smoking cigarettes, taking trashy

Insane insectivore. When my brave Boy Scout tried to cure himself of arachnophobia, he ate every small spider he encountered in one month. We do not have to go to those lengths. Just being around more bugs raises your threshold. After a few trips, it will take more than a moth to rattle you. Look away: the what-I-can't-see-can't-hurt-me method works sometimes. Condition bravery with a hefty reward. Find reasons to love your bug brethren. Convince yourself crickets are handsome and those poor mosquitoes are just famished. Okay, here are a few of my more believable rationalizations.

- Sometime in my childhood I was taught ants like to picnic. I blame *Sesame Street*. That distant memory makes it really hard to hate them. Pick one up. Look into her eyes. She's just wondering where the picnic's at.

- Primrose moths are fuzzy-headed and an unearthly yellow and pink. They're the insect I would most want to be (if I absolutely had to pick). So naturally, I kind of like them.

- Daddy longlegs pose a unique challenge because they favor cavernous places, like the space between the tent and the rain fly. I try to imagine them in top hats, kicking their elegant legs. When that doesn't work I try to remember they eat other bugs.

- Caterpillars are easy. They're undeniably cute. You can outrun them. And birds need them to survive. ❧

magazine quizzes. Work on your screenplay. Do the Sunday crossword. Knit. Those two runaway husbands who shared the GLOK space sat in their folding chairs all weekend. They didn't fish, hike, or play rummy. They just sat. They really relished their sitting. They looked like two people who looked forward to camping just for the prime sitting opportunities. City mice are seriously deprived of spacious sitting room and quiet sitting time. Give that dapper rump a rest on a primitive perch. You've got an invitation to slack. Just chill. Sit.

🐾　🐾　🐾　🐾　🐾

You're this close (imagine two fingers held microns apart) to being able to rock the backcountry. There are just a few details and matters of business to tend to, and chapter 7 makes them painless. I promise. Proper woodland etiquette, shelter construction, knot know-how, primitive precautions, vocabulary, checklists, even the truth about conquering the cat hole—it's all there. Just think, you're only one chapter away from earning your first merit badge!

Impressing the Owls

Ethics, rules, instructions, diagrams,
vocabulary, and checklists
(yes, this is the chapter on pooping).

In a misty forest in Pennsylvania smack in the middle of the day, something swooped down in front of me to a low-hanging branch. While trying to catch my breath, I began reviewing the list of reasons I'd make a terrible specimen for the aliens. The branch slowly bent and sank to eye level, and I saw that the spaceship was actually a heavy-lidded, chocolate-charcoal, ornately patterned owl. Face to face, we shared a moment. Then as suddenly as he came, my owl buddy took off, leaving me with an absurd, yet burning yen. Will we run into each other in Ohio? Will another wild wanderer flit in and out of my life? I've convinced myself owls are the mysterious guardians of the wilderness, visiting to check in on our practices. Just thinking of their dark watchful eyes keeps me in line and makes me a more responsible camper. If I'm tempted to toss a cigarette butt on the trail or wash a pot in a stream, I stop and consider what my owl guide might think.

Messing around is absolutely encouraged in the back-country, but there are still rules to follow. Some guidelines are steadfast—they're protections for both you and nature—and others are more open to interpretation. Some you'll forget as soon as you learn them and later relearn and reinvent as you go. This chapter is like the front of a mullet—all business. It's filled with hard facts, solutions, cross-referencing opportunities, diagrams, checklists, and even vocabulary. It should satisfy the need-to-know itch for all learning styles and help every girl land her own feathered mentor.

Wise Up

The United States Forest Service understands the power of a handy one-liner doled out by a cute creature. They've had Smokey Bear working for them since 1944 spreading his famous,

Owl obsession. Because of their nocturnal lifestyle, owls are often cultural taboos. They got a bum rap with the "harbinger of death and destruction" malarkey. Owls have been spotted on the arms of awesome ancient goddesses. Athena liked to take their form. I was disappointed to find Owl-Man is actually a creepy cryptozoological creature, akin to the Loch Ness Monster. Rumor has it he hung out in England in the seventies and scared people with glowing red eyes. My owl buddy sometimes appears as a half-human, but he's got hazel eyes. He's more venerable guru of good than death-mongering roadside attraction. ❦

"Only you can prevent wildfires." Then there's Woodsy, the roly-poly version of my owl buddy. His popular motto "Give a hoot, don't pollute!" has been updated to the more heartfelt, "Lend a hand—care for the land." A later, more grownup adage from the hippies didn't come with a critter but offered more refined environmental ethics: "Take only pictures, leave only footprints." There's no reason why we can't have our owl mascots to croon conservation principles in our ears. Think intuitive, insightful, possibly Buddhist, but a touch frisky too. Professor Pristine says, "Be good to nature, so it can live and last. Okay then, drinks are on me." Even if it's for selfish reasons—like you don't want to get hives when you swim in a lake or you get a kick out of watching moss grow. The places we camp aren't beautiful by accident. Everyone is, or should be, doing their part to keep them that way. Sometimes it's fun to be bad. This is not one of those instances. Littering in the backcountry is not like pilfering eye shadow from Kmart.

Codes for conscientious camping are scattered all over the Internet and plastered on posters and pamphlets. (Flip forward to the online links in the resources section, and you'll see what I mean.) Conservation groups are practically shouting through megaphones. Let's listen up. They're broadcasting "Leave No Trace" or "Tread Lightly" ethics, but our feathery sensei would call them "The Virtuous Vixens' Vows of Earth Protection." Then, with brandy snifter in one hand, he'd give us a playful pat on our collective rump with the other and . . . anyway, here goes—four ways to make sure we don't plunder the last natural wonders we've got in this modern world.

Spread the Love

Do spread the love, and not just to adorable animals—love the soil and the vegetation, and, while you're at it, the water too. Again, always camp at least two hundred feet from water, trails, and cliffs. Remember, little things matter—be conscious of where you step. Stay on the trails to minimize impact, and camp in designated or established sites. Don't plop your tent down on lush greens. The more sites we build, the more land we trample. We don't want to end up with a primitive parking lot. Keep sites small and use only what you need. Don't pillage. A "just looking" policy is best, but if you do forage, pick only a little and from dispersed areas. Fires have a big impact—take a look at the charred ground. Always build in existing rings. Use downed wood. Never chop or saw into trees. And put the fire out—all the way out.

Don't Be a Jerk to the Animals

Don't feed anything, touch anything, or tease anything. Even giving an animal a few grains of couscous could lead to its demise. People treats might be disastrous for its digestive system, or teach it to trust humans, who won't all be as nice. Try not to disrupt their lives or homes. Would you want huge armadillos to visit your apartment, feed you grubs, poke you while you're doing it, and mess up your record collection? If you invite your favorite pet on your camping trip, keep a close watch. Domestic beasts get pretty psyched about the wild. They have a knack for tracking down other animals' poop, giving ticks a free ride, and causing camping chaos.

Don't Be a Jerk to Other Humans Either

Don't worry, you'll have to put up with a lot less than you would on any day in the civilized world. When hikers meet on a narrow trail, one steps aside—it's not a game of chicken. They also say "hello"—soften that urban edge and embrace country camaraderie. If you do find yourself sharing space, be a good neighbor. Talk with your quiet voice. Don't stare. And don't leave a mess for the next campers to pick up. Take some pointers from the deluge of television crime dramas—when you leave camp, remove all evidence you were ever there. If you inherit a messy site, clean up after the previous slobs. You'll score camping karma points, redeemable in urban areas too.

Always Strive to Be an Ace Camper

Every time I camp I learn something new, or at least a way to refine my methods. Check into restrictions and know the unique conditions of the place you're headed to. Brush up on your fire skills and conservation principles. Make it easy to be responsible by bringing everything you need and staying organized. There will be less temptation to throw an apple core in a ditch if you have ample ziplock bags and everyone knows where to find them. No one wants to play hall monitor, but make sure your buddies know the deal too. The rules are simple and, even better, they make sense. Laziness is the only excuse for being a bad camper, and owls are not impressed by laziness.

The Tough Talk

I'm tired of playing the prudish mom who's avoiding explaining where babies come from to her racy teenage daughter. Yes, sooner or later you will have to poop in the backcountry. And you will use a cat hole. After trying cappuccino for the first disastrous time at sixteen, I didn't think I'd ever be forced to make a drop-off in the woods again. Nagging questions tormented me before my first outing. Would my leg muscles

Pack it in, pack it out—a primer on proper waste management. Almost anything you bring in, you've got to carry out. Thorough planning and clever repackaging will mean less trash to lug, but some garbage is unavoidable. Leftovers must be sealed in an airtight bag, kept out of reach of scavengers, and tossed out at home. That includes wrappers and cigarette butts too. Campfires must be extremely hot to completely consume bits of food and packaging. It's not unusual to find foil and plastic trash in the fire pit. Juicy Fruit fossils aren't the artifacts we want to discover on our wild excursions. Paper and cardboard are the only things you can dispose of in the flames. Reserve a pile of these for easy tinder.

Some waste can't be carried out, such as *gray* or used water. Try using the smallest possible amount of soap when washing up. Boiling water alone works well on pots, and sand, used gently, scours dishes and exfoliates faces. Everything, including your body, can get thoroughly sudsy back at home. Use biodegradable soap and avoid harsh detergents. If there's one product city girls know about, it's good cleanser. Bring some all-natural stuff or experiment with baking soda—again, give way? How could I conceal my bare behind from my cute co-camper? Would bugs attack at a crucial moment? Worse, would they settle on exposed nether regions? I'm proud to say I made it, and you will too. Only unusual folk prefer a cat hole to indoor plumbing, but it is surprisingly tolerable once you get the hang of it. Most of us ladies are already accustomed to squatting, hovering, avoiding our pants, and trying to find something to wipe with in public bathrooms, never mind our stealth skills behind bushes and down alleys. If you're already

---

it's toothpaste, scrub, and deodorizer. And don't forget a wash-basin or bucket to use as a backcountry sink. Strain any lingering chunks through a paper towel or bandana, and trash them. Then disperse the wastewater over a big area, and always two hundred feet from water sources. Even earth-friendly soap can disrupt the natural state of things.

Ladies, we've got the added hassle of female garbage. Call me a coward—I don't camp during my period. Both my brain and my body are calmer at home where there are fluffy pillows, scotch on ice, and *Three's Company* episodes on DVD. If you're brave, or just unlucky, make sure you have plenty of airtight bags. I hate to say it, but you don't want to keep opening the same bag and catching a whiff. Secure or hang all bathroom trash along with kitchen trash (and anything else smelly), sprinkle baking soda in the bag to keep odors away, and toss it out later, back in civilization. Lore about bears being attracted to the scent of unmentionables is just that, folklore. But I'd rather be overly cautious than add being mauled by bears to the list of headaches caused by my damn period. ❧

Earn It, Own It, Show It Off!

A pat on the head, a hug, a carrot, free money—who doesn't like rewards? Merit badges are delightful to make and even more delightful to give. Each GLOK was presented with an achievement badge at our reunion tapas dinner. Jen got Good Wood, for determined wood gathering; Laura, Den Diva, for ace bear-bag hanging; and Rachel, Miss Peaks, for stellar rock-climbing skills. Badges make campers smile and, subtly pinned to a tote bag, provide for effortless showing off.

> GATHER UP
> Squares of different colored felt
> Scissors
> Pretty buttons
> Sewing needle and thread
> Flat-backed craft pins or safety pins
> Superglue
> Card stock
> Hole punch
> Pen

1. Cut the felt into various shapes, between 1 1/2 and 3 inches in size. One badge could be a series of blue, green, and gray leaves; another could be pink and purple hearts. Good with scissors? Get ambitious and cut out intricate camping-themed shapes—animals, trees, tents, silhouettes of your troop's happy faces.

2. Place three or four of the cutouts on top of each other so bits of color peek out, creating an interesting, layered stack. Rest a button on top—a small button is the eye for a bird, a large button could be the center of a series of circles. This is where the layers will be connected to create the badge.

3. Sew up through the felt layers into the button's holes to fasten the layers together. Start by pushing the needle through from the back, so the knot is hidden. Sew through at least ten times, until it feels secure. Push through one of the button's holes a last time to the back, and tie off, again so the knot is hidden.

4. Attach a pin to the back of the badge with a few stitches— don't go all the way through the badge this time; just stitch it to the back.

5. Add a few tiny squirts of superglue where the stitches and felt meet the pin, and let dry.

6. Cut out a shape of card stock, bigger than the badge. Write the official badge title and the recipient's name somewhere in the corner. Punch two holes in the center and pin the badge to the card.

an outdoor pee virtuoso, you're halfway there. If not, maybe you're too good at fighting the stinging urgency. Seize the moment. Do anything that will make you keener to relieve pressure than to coddle your cold feet. Drink an extra cup of coffee. Eat oatmeal with raisins. Gnaw on raw carrots. Nothing crushes the fear of the dreaded cat hole like the desperate spasms of the lower intestine. Induce the onslaught. The best cat-hole advice: don't miss your window.

While setting up camp, keep an eye out for comfy spots to do your business. When you gotta go, you'll have one less thing standing in your way. Meander. Check behind trees and bushes. Get out of sight of camp. Choose a secluded patch of dirt at least two hundred feet away from other sites, trails, and water. When the mood is right, reach for your dependable cat-hole shovel. I hang my garden trowel conveniently next to the toilet paper and wipes. Grab your supplies and slip away from camp on the sly or invite a bathroom buddy. Although I don't delight in sharing my stinky butt, I ask a trustworthy friend to stand guard forty paces away. As long as they're sensible enough to face away, talk to you if you need it, and shut up if you need that too, a little backup is comforting in such a compromising position.

Put a cork in it. Laura ate a whole package of Kraft Cheese Slices on the ride to Kentucky and didn't go for four days. Self-constipation works, but it can't be healthy. More important, why deprive yourself of the colossal smile you'll have on your walk back to camp? Flee from sharks, tarantulas, and zombies, but not from the cat hole. You can take the cat hole. ❧

Now for the digging. There are a few classic cat-hole models. I opt for a plain pit, with about two feet of nothing around it. If a branch or leaf brushes up against me, I'm sure to scream and disrupt the process. Some people prefer a faux-toilet experience. They dig a hole directly behind a log or rock, so they can sit and aim off the back. Another favored way is to dig one or two feet behind a standing tree. Then squat, latch hold of the trunk, and slam-dunk. I fancy a hands-off squat. With my trowel jammed in the ground right in front of me, I can grab on if my balance falters. You don't have to be a sharpshooter. A proper cat hole is six to eight inches deep and four to six inches wide—there's room for error. (Two exceptions: on the beach and in the desert a shallow cat hole is preferred so the sun can aid in decomposition.) Clear away sticks and rocks, and dig in. Now, with the bravery it takes to tear off a Band-Aid, drop your drawers and go for it. If you've come prepared for action, all should go quickly and smoothly. Don't look down. Bugs might come by to catch the show, and glimpsing the audience before the finale can be a sure showstopper. Keep your eyes locked on the panoramic view.

Cat-hole cache. Pack incidentals to make your movements as painless as possible. On the bathroom tree at camp I hang my shovel right next to a plastic grocery bag filled with: a few more bags (grocery and ziplock), thin toilet paper (less bulk to lug back), baby wipes, baby powder, and bug spray (to keep the flying opportunists away). Add a copy of *Tiger Beat*, a lucky rabbit's foot, a nip of tequila—whatever might soothe, distract, and loosen up those muscles. ❧

Once the deed is done, take it easy. It's pretty much business as usual. Every time I visit the backcountry loo, I carry my cat-hole cache. Used paper and wipes go in their own bag, and before I dress, I treat my rear to a light dusting of powder. Then do the backcountry flush—fill in the hole with the displaced dirt, leaves, and rocks. Stand a stick up to mark the spot, so fellow campers don't step into a booby trap or, worse, dig their own cat hole there. And walk away with a clear conscience, a clean behind, and a spring in your step. Mastering the cat hole is second only to building a kick-ass fire for feeling like you've got this camping thing down. Encourage hesitant poopers. Spread the word: the cat hole purrs like a kitten.

Fear of the infamous hole should never stop you from camping. Not quite as persuasive as a bidet, the following gadgets are at least convincing starts for reluctant poopers. Collapsible plastic toilet seats cost less than $20 and weigh only three pounds. Simply place it over your cat hole for that familiar homey feel. Or go one step up with the hunter's folding toilet bowl. It's bigger than a breadbox (maybe equally difficult to pack), but it does lift you up, away from the ground. It comes with a bag for packing out poops, but I suggest trashing the bag. Cut the bottom out and line it up over the cat hole. Better yet, construct your own toilet box out of liquor-store surplus. (Tell them you need the boxes for moving.) Use only cardboard, toss the remains in the campfire (be sure it burns down to ashes), and lighten your homeward-bound load (in more ways than one). ☙

Gimme Shelter

Making our way down the rough-and-ready chick checklist, right under Poop in a Cat Hole is Erect a Lean-To. A camping lean-to is simply a handmade hiding spot with a sloping roof. Sneak away from the sun's watchful eye, but still catch the breeze. Stir up fettuccini alfredo on the stove and out of the reach of pelting rain. Lean-tos are usually constructed with rope and a tarp, but even shoelaces and a garbage bag can make a shelter in a pinch. A lean-to can be tall enough for standing under or a low storage area for storing supplies. I like to have enough space to sit comfortably—if the lightning decides to put on a special display, I've got a dry front-row seat. Rigging can be as simple as stretching four tarp corners between well-situated trees, or it can require a little ingenious fiddling. Think logically and improvise. Use anything available—a huge tropical leaf, a poncho, duct tape—and any technique you dream up. Tailor these examples for your space and supplies to construct your ideal cozy cabana or cocktail veranda.

First, let's imagine the stars are aligned—you remembered to pack your sturdy tarp, and there are plenty of convenient trees to tie onto. You could whip up a tent, minus the doors and floor. String a rope, at your height, between two trees that are about the length of your tarp apart. Drape the tarp over the rope as if you're drying it on a clothesline. Pull it even on both sides. Weigh the corners down with rocks, or stick tent stakes through the tarp grommets. Voila! For something a little more ambitious and less confining, don't center the tarp

Lean on me—a few more lean-to lessons.

- Where should you hang? Which way is the rain coming from? Where's the wind blowing? Face it toward the fire and be cozy. Place it near the tent door for a dry passageway. Assess the particular needs of the day— and remember, there's no disgrace in having to rehang.

- Tarps have handy grommets (like shower curtain holes but reinforced with metal) to tie onto. When working with a plain sheet of plastic, wrap up a stone in each corner, making a little package. Tie the rope onto the stone packages to stop it from slipping.

- Remember, nylon rope is easier to work with than polyester, cotton, or manila, and the ends can be melted with a lighter to stop fraying. Look for pinky-thick, braided rope—and whatever you do, don't forget to pack a few lengths of rope on every trip, including one at least twenty feet long for your bear bag.

- A flat roof is just a bucket for rain to collect in. Always give your shelter's roof a jaunty slope.

- Are you a postmodern camper? Some campers bring extra tent poles and stakes for their lean-to; others construct thatch roofs out of branches. Follow any school you fancy and play architect.

- Hang your tarp while the sun shines. The point is to be ready when a storm strikes, not to get soaked trying to get it up during a downpour. 🐾

over the rope. Pull it farther down on one side, and secure the
long bottom with a row of rocks or a log. Keep about three
feet of tarp hanging over the other side. Tie two more lengths
of rope, long enough to reach the ground, to the corner grommets. Pull the ropes away and toward the ground, as if you
were giving the lean-to arms. Tie the ends to stakes and pound
them in. These are guylines, and this is a traditional lean-to
form. It's the kind of snug spot you can imagine sitting under
to ponder the percussion of raindrops. Any variation on this
rope-tarp-tree-stake-rock-log system will work. Duct-tape a
split garbage bag over the front for a doorway. Add two more
sides by layering on another tarp. Tie the guylines to nearby
trees. As long as your roof is angled and the tarp secure, you
give good shelter.

What happens if you encounter uncooperative trees or
you're on a treeless beach or desert? This highly provisional system makes for a small, shady hideaway. All you need are two
sturdy branches of equal length and at least three feet long, a
heavy-duty lawn-style garbage bag, and two weighty things, like
rocks or water jugs. First, cut or tear the bag down one of its
seams to double the surface area. Unfold the bag and make small
holes on the adjacent corners of one of the short sides. Stand the
branches in the soil or sand the short width of the bag apart.
Secure the sticks by digging in deep and covering with plenty
of soil. Pull the corner bag holes snugly over the tips of the
branches. Lay the length of the bag out over the ground, and
weigh down the corners with rocks, jugs, or anything heavy.
For more security, run guylines down from the tops of the

branches to the ground. Tie them to smaller sticks or stakes, and dig in. It's a bit more like a disposable hide-and-seek spot than a sanctuary, but it works.

Tie One On

Shelter building is knot-intensive. Campers know their knots. They're a tradition, an art form, and a necessity. Attach a sleeping bag to your pack, rig up a tarp, hang clothesline, and play bondage games. Knot tying is a nifty practical skill. Stage hands, jewelry makers, sailors, seamstresses, farmers, and hairdressers all tie knots. *The Ashley Book of Knots*, the definitive guide, cites almost four thousand examples. Camping knots are precise and plain. Some are prized for strength and others for their ability to be tied and untied easily. I always triple-knotted my Ms. Pac-Man laces into a tangled disaster that my mom had to cut off every few months. This kind of clumsy cord work won't do when you need to be able to attach and release efficiently. If you weren't one of those nimble-fingered lanyard-loving fifth-grade girls, you can get by on two basic knots. Gather up about five feet of pinky-thick nylon rope and practice till perfect. Don't worry, I won't leave you hanging. Flip to the diagrams if you forget which knot is good for clothesline and which might lash a shifty prisoner to a tree.

Square Knot

Let's get one thing straight: you already know the overhand knot. It's the pre–bunny ears tie we all do every time we tie our shoes. Now that that's settled, the square knot, a handsome fellow, is really two overhand knots made right on top of each other. The only catch is to reverse the order—if the first tie is right over left, the second is left over right, or vice versa.

1. For practicing purposes, wrap the rope around your leg, or even a pillow. Pull the ends even.

2. Make one overhand knot—cross the ends over, loop one end under, and pull.

3. Now, tie another one, but loop the opposite end under, and pull. There it is, a square knot. Isn't it elegant? To loosen, push the ends toward each other, and the knot buckles and opens.

Why bother? This is *the* knot for attaching anything substantial to your pack (sleeping bag, sleeping pad, tent poles)—something you'll probably do on every trip. It's easy to untie, and it won't slip under strain.

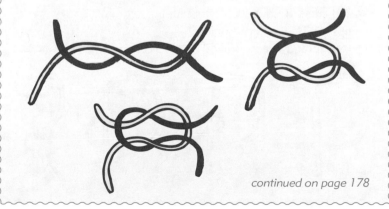

continued on page 178

continued from page 177

Tautline Hitch

This knot is a bit more advanced, but it is hands down the handiest. Its beauty is its adjustability. Pulled one way, it slides to give or take slack; pulled another, it won't budge.

1. Wrap the rope around a table leg, or even a person, to practice this one. Give yourself two feet to work with on one side and leave the other side long.

2. Take the short end and go under the long end, making a big loop.

3. Take that same short end, drop it into the loop, and come back out.

4. Take the short end again, drop it in again, but this time bring the end under the long end and through the new loop you just created.

5. Pull it tight. You'll see that the knot slides along the long piece. This is how you adjust for more or less slack when, for example, heavy wet towels put a strain on your clothesline.

Why bother? Because this knot can pull off almost anything a camper demands—hang a bear bag or clothesline, secure things to trees, run guylines to stakes. Definitely buddy up to this one.

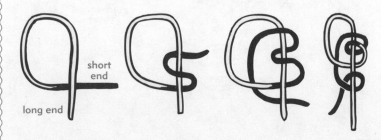

Stuck with Two Shorties

Here's an easy way to turn two short pieces into one longer cord.

1. Lay the two pieces on top of each other. Line up one set of the ends.

2. Now, treating them as if they were one rope, make a loop in the lined-up ends. Pull the knot tight.

3. Take one of the unknotted ends in each hand, separate them, and pull apart. The knot connecting them will lock in place.

Why bother? This isn't a knot to rely on when rappelling down a wall, but it will get the tarp hung between two long-distance trees. ☙

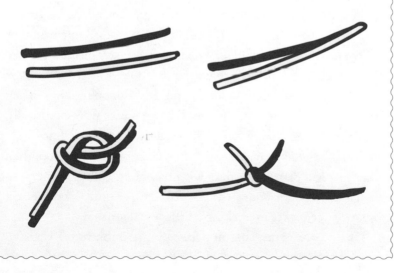

Primitive Preparedness

Woodland-loving sex maniacs, bears with a taste for Kiehl's moisturizer, aliens on a mission to probe young things with great haircuts, tipsy hunters' stray bullets—the GLOK had a long list of camping fears. The whole trip nearly went kaput when the local agencies I phoned up were fuzzy on the exact dates of hunting season. Emails trickled in, timidly suggesting we cancel. (I can only imagine what was said in the emails that I wasn't sent.) There is no doubt city folk are raised on heaping spoonfuls of suspicions about the country, peppered with sensational news stories of wilderness abductions. But camping anxiety is just like any fear of the unknown—get to know it, and the fear fades. Once you return in one (supercharged) piece from your first trip, you'll get a break from pastoral paranoia.

That said, it never hurts to be prepared. The GLOK had a plan. Laura, who took a self-defense course in college, was ready to use her kung fu grip. Jen brought the sharpest knife from her kitchen, which we hid under a rock so the closest girl could make a dash for it. Rachel kept a dagger strapped to her leg (mostly because it made her feel slick), and I hid pepper spray in my pocket. In retrospect, our Power Ranger antics were pretty silly, but at the time it felt good to be proactive. You won't find yourself in a knife fight with toothless backwoods bumpkins either, but having a plan for dealing with basic backcountry emergencies is solid policy. Know the possible dangers and the solutions. Knowledge makes everything a little less daunting.

Here are some common camping troubles and ways to deal. Think of it as a game of "What If?"

Don't Play Dead

Check the dates of hunting season. Are rifles allowed, or will it be arrows aimed at your heart? If the thought of being that close to firing guns makes you uncomfortable, it's okay to reschedule. If you do go, wear plenty of bright orange—coordinated fluorescent bandanas solidified the GLOK's fantasy of being a team of sexy superheroes. The goal is to be as unlike a furry animal as possible. Cover your head in Day-Glo, and pin, tie, or sew bright fabric to packs and clothes. Stick to the trails and make some human noises so there's less of a chance of being mistaken for prey.

Batten Down the Hatches

The sky may grow dim and gray, an earthy smell rises up, and sometimes a wind blows through—secure your campsite if a storm is brewing. Tie down and cover everything valuable. Bring plenty of goodies to hole up with, but don't even consider cooking in the tent. Raw pasta is much better than burning tent. Catch the lightning extravaganza from a safe spot. Sit on a sleeping bag for extra insulation. Stay away from anything standing lone and tall—a singular huge tree or boulder. Avoid open fields and high elevations. And get out of the water. In the forest, the safest place is under a patch of short trees or bushes. At the beach or desert, seek out a low nook. Wait the worst of it out in the safest possible place. Regroup and reemerge when the sky is bright and the birds sing again.

Tried and True (Almost): Leaves of Three, Let it Be

There are always annoying exceptions. Poison sumac can have seven to thirteen leaflets. A rabbit could chew up one telltale leaf, making only two. Take it from me, paranoia can make any plant look poisonous. Don't freak. Though I'm covered in eczema all summer long, I've yet to catch anything from a plant. The first line of defense is long pants and tall socks. To help in identification, look for small white (poison ivy) or yellow (poison oak) berries. Poison sumac, the worst but also the rarest, grows mostly in boggy areas and has yellow or cream-colored berries. Want to be extra cautious? Invest in an ivy block, kind of like sun block. If you do brush up against an unfriendly plant, be careful not to touch anything with the affected skin. Wash up right away with cold water and alcohol (something most good first aid kits will include). Carefully remove any affected clothes and bag them up for the wash (or the trash) back home. Calamine lotion, baking powder paste, or cortisone cream will soothe and dry, but more severe rashes may need a doctor's attention. The nastiest trick these plants play is when they're thrown into a campfire. The poison can be inhaled and actually cause a rash in your mouth, throat, and lungs. Antihistamines might help, but why suffer needlessly? If your encounter with one of the poisonous three is particularly painful or intense, scrap the trip, call a doctor, and spend the rest of your vacation on the couch.

Attack of the Fifty-Foot Scorpion!

Tales of venomous creatures are more legend than reality. Rattlesnakes, brown recluse spiders, and scorpions do exist, but they usually run away from people, not toward them. To them we're evil predators, not delicious prey. Be careful and you'll be less likely to provoke an attack. Watch where you sit and walk. Make some noise to give critters a chance to slither or scamper away. Snakes like to lie in the sun. They're partial to rocks and retreat to the nooks between boulders and logs. Spiders and scorpions prefer dark hidden places. Check inside your shoes before you put them on. Shake out any blankets or clothes you laid on the ground. Carefully flip rocks, logs, and the tent (when breaking camp); you could startle a napping crawly. Remedies for serious bites are just as fabled as the stories of the bites themselves. Don't go sucking on wounds to remove poison. Make a thorough note of what the assailant looked like (size, color, markings) and head to an emergency room right away.

Bugger Off

Any traumatizing run-ins with insects should be taken seriously, but particularly distressing are ticks. Actually, it's inaccurate to call ticks bugs or insects. Those creepy parasites are arachnids. Just thinking about them makes my neck itch. They're so damn tiny, and the flurry of Lyme disease reports is downright scary. Cover up before hikes, especially when traipsing through tall grass or brush. Mist with bug juice— unfortunately, the harsh chemical stuff (DEET) works best against ticks. Most important, perform thorough and frequent tick checks. They love warm hidden areas—behind ears, in armpits, on bellies and backs, under hair. They roam around before they dig in. Catch them early enough and you can pick and flick. If the runt has already embedded in the skin, the best way to remove it is with tweezers. Grab close to the skin and pull. Be sure to get the whole thing—it's best to even take a little skin with it too. Don't twist, crush, or break the tick's body—that could release any disease it might carry. Wash the area and the tweezers with antiseptic (again, in a decent first aid kit) and try to save the tick to show a doctor. Not all ticks cause Lyme disease, but they can carry other harmful diseases. Deer ticks or black-legged ticks—the ones that carry Lyme—are usually no bigger than the head of a pin. Other ticks can be as big as a pencil eraser. Some are hard-bodied, others soft; some brown, some red, others black or even gray. They all have eight legs, just like spiders, and little pinching barbs coming out of their heads. Tick bites can cause odd symptoms weeks after they're removed. A round, bull's-eye rash is a sure sign to see a doctor, but it's best to play it safe and check with a doctor any time you're bitten by a tick.

Keep Your Filthy Paws off My Silky Drawers

Good news: most bears don't eat people. Still, it's best to steer clear of wild animals. Not just bears, but raccoons, boar, even deer can become violent if fed, teased, or approached. Keep a meticulously clean camp, secure or hang food and trash, and most likely you won't have any party crashers. Brown and black bears, different from the notorious grizzlies, are scattered throughout the United States, anywhere they can find a suitable habitat. If you manage to get up close and personal, stay calm. Most bears can be easily frightened away by loud showy displays—stomping, yelling, banging. Clang pots together and bellow. Take a few backward steps away until you're a good distance apart. Most likely the bear will lumber off before you get far. In the face of a persistent bear, or a mom with cubs, slowly back away. Don't make eye contact, but don't turn and run. In the off chance of an attack, there are two options: keep pepper spray handy and know how to use it, or lie in a fetal position with your arms and hands covering your face. Sounds crazy but it works. Most bears will give up, or just paw you a bit, which is a welcome alternative to ending up as dinner. Truth is, bear attacks are extremely uncommon. I've only glimpsed a few bear behinds, as they hightail it away. Grizzly bears are another story. Grizzlies are found from Canada down into Wyoming—challenging camping territory. I wouldn't pitch my tent on grizzly turf unless I felt I had earned the grade of master outdoorswoman.

Is There a Doctor in the Tent?

Wouldn't it be great if we could carry tiny medics in our backpacks? There's a voluminous amount of information to know to help someone who's wounded. I carry my first aid kit, a little bit of know-how, and a lot of hope. I also bring along a camp medical guidebook if I'll be camping farther than three miles from the car. And I would certainly include a first aid course in my preparation for a long backpacking trek. For most weekend jaunts you can get by on a basic camping first aid kit, good judgment, and plain old caution. Some mishaps are treatable on the trail, others are clearly not. If you've got any doubt, seek profes-

Be a safety girl. A stocked first aid kit is a must on your camping trip. Don't forget to bring anything from your medicine cabinet you normally use, or even might use. Be prepared to save the day—get CPR certified, learn the Heimlich, or become a lifeguard. Safety skills are just as much an asset in a roller-skating rink, an airplane, or a diner as they are in the backcountry. 🐾

sional help. Reschedule, rather than regret something later. In any backcountry emergency, stay calm so you can think clearly. Then, take charge. Be the girl with a plan, and make it happen.

Get Wise Glossary

Impressing the owls is one thing; impressing other campers is another. The backcountry crowd is a proud bunch. They occasionally dabble in reverse snobbery. "I'm tough because I slept in an aluminum foil cocoon in hollowed-out snow." "Hail to me, I built a lean-to out of the bits of bramble I collected in the wind." Being able to talk shop is nice, but feeling like a legitimate camper has nothing to do with speaking the vernacular. I still refer to my tent vestibule as a porch and can't pronounce *cairn*. But lingo is fun and so is being a know-it-all. Here's some vocabulary to throw around at the next woodland cocktail party.

BACKCOUNTRY Where the call of the wild beckons you, babe.

BACKPACKING A term with some discrepancies—in the strictest sense, it refers to through-hikers on a journey who only stay in a site briefly and move on. (I call myself a *primitive camper*, but feel free to use *backpacker* if you like the sound of it. Sticklers, shmicklers.)

BANNOCK Classic camping bread; can be baked, fried, grilled, or boiled—yummy!

BEAR BAG Bag used to store food and trash out of the reach of bears (and other beasties), usually waterproof.

BLAZE A sign or marker indicating a trail, usually on a tree or a rock, often a colored splotch of paint.

BOOK TIME A rough estimate from a trail guidebook on how long a trail might take.

BUSHWHACKING Hiking off trail, discouraged for the damage it does to the wild.

CAIRN An interesting stack of rocks made by hikers to mark a trail.

CARABINER A metal ring with a latch, usually used for climbing; cheapo ones are great for attaching things (like a cup) to the outside of your pack.

CAR CAMPING Camping in a campground with the car nearby, usually within a few feet.

CAT HOLE No need to define—this one is forever burnt in our minds.

DAYPACK A small backpack for day excursions from camp (follow the super-easy directions for a handmade recycled denim daypack on pages 66–7).

FIRE RING A circle of rocks surrounding a pit in which it's safe to build a fire; also *rock ring*.

FUEL Bigger dead branches and logs, from pepperoni to pork roast size, used once a campfire is well under way; slower burning and perfect for cooking.

GIARDIA The most common microorganism to wreak havoc on campers' digestive tracts if water isn't properly purified.

GRAY WATER The water left over from washing dishes or bodies, which must be dispersed widely to minimize environmental impact.

GUYLINES Ropes coming from a tarp or tent securing it; they can be affixed to a tree or tied down with a stake.

KINDLING Pretzel-sized, small, thin, dead wood used in the early stages of fire building.

LEAN-TO Makeshift shelter with a sloped roof and three or fewer sides.

MUG-UP The last drink of the night before the fire is put out. (A big Canadian thing, and since Canadian things are usually pretty cool, I thought I should include it).

NO-SEE-UM Tiny gnats that can barely be seen, hence the name; vicious attackers.

RAIN FLY A tent's raincoat; an outer piece of removable waterproof fabric usually attached with snaps or Velcro and staked down.

TINDER The light, super-flammable stuff used to start the fire: tiny twigs, leaves, bark, paper.

VESTIBULE Covered area outside the tent door; great for keeping things dry, storing shoes, and sitting under to smoke cigarettes.

Get It Together

Finally, here are the handy dandy checklists I've been promising. Remember, some of this stuff is a necessity (flashlight), some is up for grabs (shorts or skirts), and some is totally optional (wristwatch). These are my basic lists (no espresso maker here), foundations for you to tailor. Some of this stuff

Gear

Tent*—count all the stakes before you go

Sleeping bag or blanket

Backpack

Daypack

Water purifier, filter, or tablets*

Canteen and/or 1 or 2 water bottles

Tarp*

Aluminum foil—at least a few sheets

Bug repellent*

Camping shovel*

Citronella candles*

Cloth gloves

Duct tape*

First aid kit*—don't forget personal additions

Flashlights—2 or 3; check the batteries, and don't forget extras

Matches, lighters, or other fire starters—stash at least 4 or 5

Paper towels*—1 roll for every two people is more than enough

Dishrags/bandanas—4 or 5 should do

Plastic bags*— 5 garbage bags, 5 grocery bags, 10 ziplock
    bags is my basic formula for two campers

Pocketknife*—or a kitchen knife substitute, plus a can opener
    and cork screw

Rope*—pinky-thick nylon, a few lengths, one at least twenty
    feet long

Wristwatch*

Whistle

*Group or shared gear.   *continued on page 190*

continued from page 189

Toiletries

Biodegradable soap—
1 twelve-ounce bottle
is enough for two for all
washing needs*

Baby wipes

Baby powder

Lotion with sunscreen

Hand sanitizer

Mouthwash

Birth control

Baking soda*

Cornstarch*

Face powder

Lip balm

Tweezers

Toilet paper—
1 roll for two*

Toothbrush

Towel

Kitchen

Stove*

Fuel*—double-check
supply

Soup pot or pan, or both*

Dishes—1 for eating,
1 for cutting

Cup

Spoons/forks/sporks—
1 per person, plus
1 extra for stirring and
serving

Knife

Washbasin or bucket*

Miscellaneous

Maps and guidebooks

Cell phone

Camera

Primitive party supplies—
my journal, pen, cards,
books, tape recorder,
ukulele, Frisbee, water
guns, beach ball . . .

*Group or shared gear.

(marked with an asterisk) serves the whole group—remember, each person shouldn't be weighed down by her own stove or tarp. These supplies cover a typical weekend trip in warmer weather. Modify for longer excursions or more challenging conditions. Happy packing!

That's all there is to it! Seven little chapters and you're ready to get out there and pitch your tent. Camping is easy. It's also surprising, thrilling, challenging, wild, raw, refreshing, replenishing, enlightening, blissful, exciting, jazzy, luminous, larkish, and lots of other juicy adjectives. It's downright addictive.

🐾 🐾 🐾 🐾 🐾

Once you get started, you may find yourself jonesing for some primitive reprieve back home. Chapter 8 offers up my tricks for stalking wild experiences in the concrete jungle. (Pssst—reluctant gals may want to try out these easy steps before taking the primitive plunge.)

When Hermit Crabs Attack

Ideas for getting a primitive fix at home in the big city.

During my more chaotic past life I once woke up at 4 A.M. to a man scaling our third-floor fire escape. Every night for six days straight my roommate's boyfriend tried this pathological attempt to mend their failing relationship. He was a drinker, and his effort did little more than to drive her into the arms of a bottle of rum. These two drunken sailors assaulted me from all angles. Her hysterical crying stormed my room through our flimsy walls, and his scrawny King Kong impersonation pounded through the glass. That same week my dragon boss threw me a rare bone in the form of a significant project—only, I suspected, so she could have the pleasure of watching me fall on my ass.

Something had to be done to save my fragile sanity. On day five of the onslaught I stomped into a huge discount store. I bought a fuchsia lounge chair, a novel with a Fabio look-alike on the cover, ten supposedly soothing lavender-scented candles, and an armful of chocolate donuts and salt and vinegar chips. I left a note on the coffee table that read "Consider me gone." Even if there was an offer for free sushi delivered by a sweaty young bike messenger, I was not to be interrupted. I hid out on the back porch with my arsenal of relaxation supplies, a blanket, and a cooler filled with beer. One Corona later and only thirty-five pages down, I passed out. A sore back woke me way too early, but I did manage to catch the tail end of sunrise.

Back then I had never set foot inside a tent, walked on a backcountry trail, or given camping a second thought. All I knew was I needed to skip out, to camp out. The porch retreat quenched me like a bucket of water dumped over a flea-ridden dog in heat. I recommend every maxed-out girl give it a whirl. Buy a lounge chair with drink holders on the arms. Unplug everything. Demand to be left alone (and mean it). Gather guilty pleasures. Pack the perfect cooler and flee to your own private island.

Getting primitive doesn't always have to be reserved for the perfect outdoor setting. Let's face it, modern, ambitious, and fabulous come at a steep price. All this striving to be extraordinary is exhausting. Rewarding jobs with the bonus of damaging jaw clenching. Prestigious assignments that tie up sixty hours a week. Sick days that keep getting used up with actually being sick.

Say you don't have a porch? Use someone else's, the roof, or the backyard. Or be really resourceful and build a cubby of solitude in a spare closet or even under your desk. ❧

Memos and invites piling up in multiple email accounts. Shifts to cover and ideas to run by Google. To purge our toxic woes, we require both big leaps and regular rituals. I admit, not much releases my caged kitty like camping, but sometimes there's no time to get away or there's not even a spare dime for gas. Maybe there's no car to borrow. Slight agoraphobia could creep in, leaving us unable to go anywhere. Other times we need just a nibble to hold us over between outings. Camping has schooled me in the value of primitive pleasure. Now I hunt it down, schedule it, and create my own little opportunities for roughing it even in the civilized world. Let's make a city-girl pact to take simple breathers before our eyes glaze over and we have the urge to murder the next person who smells funny on the train.

Ten Tiny Tricks for Coaxing out the Mountain Mama in the Middle of the Metropolis

These ideas are designed to distill some of the pleasures we get in the backcountry. They're small daily practices, weekly rituals, and occasional experiments for a little wild respite in the confines of the urban jungle.

Goin' on a picnic and I'm bringing asparagus, bouillabaisse, corn dogs, and dandelion salad. Seek nearby refuge and revel in the luxury of a cooler filled with ice. Pack it with all the treats the backcountry forbids. My icebox stash would include brie and baby cheesecakes. And as for treats of the nondairy variety— pickled eggs, spicy tuna rolls, and Pinot Grigio are musts. ❧

1. Scout out the Natural in the Synthetic

Untouched wilderness is awesome, but sometimes wild things thriving in the unlikeliest places are also inspiring. Sprigs of green can sprout through cracks in concrete, reminding us of how everything is adaptable. Storm water gushes down gutters, working relentlessly to make things fresh and new. Sweet blueberries grow in busy highway medians as offerings to the brave. Jot notes, make sketches, take snapshots of your finds for reassurance on a particularly unnatural afternoon. It's comforting to know we're not the only ones trying to make it in the big city.

2. Get Your Hands Dirty

Camping chores feel good because they're what old fogies call honest work, work that makes you feel tangibly useful in a way working with paper doesn't. It's work that tuckers you out rather than wears you down. Find a hands-on project and dig in. Build a shelf. Grow an herb garden for your window. Darn holes yourself instead of running to the tailor. Share your blood, sweat, and tears with the community. Paint sets for a local nonprofit theater. Help a neighbor move. Pitch in to turn

---

Remember, not all stresses come from work. Party life is demanding. There are shows you must see, boys to scope out, sales to catch. A girl can develop an affliction that my friend calls FOMS—'fraid of missing something. There's no known cure. Grit your teeth and turn down an invitation once in a while in favor of some nourishing quiet time. ❧

an abandoned lot into a garden. At the end of the day you'll crack open an icy cold one knowing you're worth your salt.

3. Spell Pretzel

It's not uncommon to see folks of all shapes and sizes bending and extending this way and that when they emerge from their tents. Camping makes bodies want to reach. We stretch because we feel good, and then stretching makes us feel even better. Do it outdoors or near a window. Bend over and contemplate the ground. Now go the other way and wink at the sun. Shake off the poor desk posture. Sit cross-legged and visualize your next campfire. Stretching soothes restless muscles and minds. How many palindromes can your limbs spell?

4. Take Your Problems to the Primates

When you can't make it to the wilderness to visit the animals in their own habitats, then call on them at the local zoo. Watching two monkeys solve a dispute over a banana with a hug is a sure reality check. Hate the human tyranny of cages

Give me an F! Give me a U! There are a lot of good reasons I never made the cheerleading squad. Peppy people make me uncomfortable. How can I take the advice of someone who is centered, productive, and happy when I'm (occasionally) a miserable disaster? Rest assured, these suggestions come from a lover of destructive behavior. The bags under my eyes and journals brimming with lists of things that piss me off prove it. So quit whining and try this stuff. Better yet, make up your own. ❧

and gawking crowds? Save a school of fish from the pet store while you activate your chi (according to feng shui believers, anyway). Watch the underwater drama unfold. Witness the miracle of life and embrace the grief of the inverted floater. Seek solutions to warm-blooded dilemmas by staring into the shimmering cold-blooded world.

5. Let Some Air under Your Dress

It has always been a fantasy of mine to run rampant in a gorgeous dress; sometimes I stuff one into my backpack. I can't possibly be alone in this. Music videos are built on this potent image. In the backcountry we get to hike up our skirts and crawl

---

Close but no cigar. Here's the lazy girl's guide to getting back to nature without moving a muscle—stuff to watch, read, and hear that's kinda sorta like the real thing.

Watch. *Baraka*—chill out to luscious time-lapse nature photography.

Milo and Otis or *Homeward Bound*—furry, sweet, and wonderfully bucolic.

Caveman—a ridiculous but irresistible farce of primitive life starring Ringo Starr.

Mosquito Coast—my favorite tale of going uncivilized, starring two great thespians, River Phoenix and Harrison Ford.

Read. *In My Tent*—one of the prettiest children's books I never read as a kid and one of the sweetest portrayals of camping ever. I own two copies now.

Prodigal Summer—Barbara Kingsolver captures the feminine and sensual in nature and is sure to spark pastoral passion.

around in the dirt just like people in sensible pants. Back home, put on a pink ruffled number and run around the park. Make a mud pie. Change a tire. Sort the recycling, all in a completely inappropriate demure frock. And don't pay too much attention to how the hem falls. Be a brazen flurry of frills. Bring the paradox of the can-do girly girl home with you.

6. Get Cosmic

I've slept under my share of plastic novelty glow-in-the-dark stars. Except for a persistent addiction to rope rugs, I'm over shabby dorm decor, but astronomy is cool. After just one camping trip you'll be lamenting the limited city sky. So give it the

Watership Down—my favorite case of anthropomorphism. Who can resist talking bunnies?

Walden or *Wild Fruits*—I'm partial to these two, but anything by Henry David Thoreau is mandatory nature reading and a refreshing perspective for denizens of the modern world.

Listen. John Denver—the quintessential Boy Scout—always has me humming about the simple life.

Will Oldham—another good ol' country boy I dream of following down rural routes.

Tori Amos and Cat Power—singing that takes me floating on meandering rivers.

Devendra Banhart—a soundtrack for stargazing or even imaginary stargazing.

Kimya Dawson—*the* girl with the guitar I'd most like to have 'round the campfire. Her songs get me working on my ideal camping trip guest list. ❧

old college try and head up to the roof on a clear night. Drive out to the suburbs where less light drowns out the stars. If that doesn't work, recreate the immaculate backcountry view with a miniature planetarium. For about $35 you can project accurate constellations at home. They're much more romantic, interesting, and—dare I say—classy than the sticky variety. Dim the lights, skip the Pink Floyd, charge admission, and make back your investment.

7. Sip Some Water in the Sun

When it gets warm enough my neighbor sits on her stoop almost every day. She reads, eats, and talks on the phone out there. As I fulfill the duties of my hectic life, I walk by and smile, but I secretly envy, even dislike her. How does she find the time to loll around? The answer is, she makes it. Sometimes it seems

Water-break beats. As a lover of lists I couldn't help keeping a tally of the musings the drink brings. Unless I'm particularly preoccupied, they're decidedly unlike the thoughts crossing my mind all day. Mostly the lists read like a document of my neighborhood. "I think Norris can see in my bedroom window from his kitchen." "The trees out front are shorter than the ones on the two adjacent streets." "How can Jessica eat pizza day in and day out and still be so skinny?" You don't have to be a journal keeper to make a water-break journal. You just have to be a nosey snooper. Compile your scathing realizations in an anonymous neighborhood newsletter or hang onto them for a hysterical rainy-day read. ❧

I can only get my legs and brain to slow down when I get out into the wild. All my previous attempts to get myself to enjoy the outdoors for a few minutes every day have failed. Except this one. Force yourself to drink sixteen ounces of water outside. That's just one bottle. Do it on a balcony, the steps of a bank, a park bench. Plop down wherever you can. I picked water because it fits with the whole healthy thing, but drink sixteen ounces of anything. It works better than giving yourself a time limit because it lets your mood set the pace. Plus there's no pressure of a clock to check. Gulp it down or savor each sip. It's like taking a walk to the bizzarro water cooler.

It's easy being green. Color theorists say green is easiest on our eyes and reminds us of growth and harmony—just one of the reasons the backcountry is so soothing. Why not try creating some green goodness at home? They say working in a garden is like meditating, but if you haven't got outdoor space try creating a bathroom safari. The plants will soak up the steam and giggle at the singing in the shower. A green cocoon makes bathroom routines more relaxing. Throw in leopard-print towels and a zebra shower curtain, and every flush becomes an outback expedition. Extra kudos to the ladies with a green thumb; plants inexplicably wither in my care. Horticulture befuddles you too? Fake stuff is difficult to murder. Plastic flowers and nylon grass may be worth your gaining a reputation as an eccentric biddy. City dwellers pay big bucks to cover their roofs with the perfect piece of imposter lawn, and designers construct gowns out of the grassy fur. If that's too much kitsch to handle, get a cactus; they don't mind much abuse either. 🐾

8. Turn out the Lights

See how many hours you can spend without the luxuries of technology. Let yourself wake up without the alarm. Skip the shower. Use only natural light. Don't even consider the computer. Walk or ride a bike. Don't drive a car or even take the train. It's one thing to rough it in the backcountry, but it's another when you're surrounded by tempting conveniences. Can you beat the urge to blow-dry?

9. Plant a Plastic Tree

When I was cleaning offices for extra money I'd bump the computer mice so I could sneak a peek at people's desktop vistas: hilly pastures with grazing cows, tumbling cliff waterfalls, quaint cobblestone roads. I learned that almost everyone yearned to be somewhere else, somewhere more rustic. Even my extremely citified late great-grandmother had a poster of a bland stand of birch trees in her kitchen. Maybe all the artificial trappings we're so quick to write off as cheesy actually do some good. Hang a canopy of fake leaves and flowers over your bed and dream of the jungle. Drift off while you dress—cover every visible inch of space in your closet with a tropical island collage. Throw a piece of Astroturf down on the patio to give your toes some green to meet. Create a fantasy view of anything, anywhere. The best part is it doesn't have to be remotely realistic. Float away with a recording of ocean waves while gazing at a mural of the sunset over a desert horizon.

10. Get Geeky

Campers know that the magic of the universe quiets the mind and quells the crazies. Go back to nature and transcend the superficial bogus crap. Errands, schedules, and facades shrivel when faced with the straightforward natural world. Unwavering facts are a welcome hiatus from uncertainty and rumination. Rent a science documentary, watch the Discovery Channel, or reach for an old textbook. Brush up on biology and get a crash course in how uncomplicated life can be. Watch a hyena devour a zebra calf, only to be later chomped on by a lion, and realize life's too short to worry about which pair of jeans makes you look like Kate Moss. Read up on the polygamous mating practices of seals and stop fretting over whether or not he'll call. (At least he's most likely not out romancing fifty other ladies.) Besides, having a library of science knowledge at your fingertips is both useful and sexy. Talk nerdy to me, baby.

Hail, Hail the Gang's All Here . . .

How about sharing some of this newfound savagery with your fellow city slickers? From defecating in a dirt hole to waking up with uncontrollable sleeping-bag hair, the nitty-gritty of camping makes for honest-to-goodness bonding. City life, on the other hand, can be so full and frenzied we tend to orbit around each other, hardly ever crashing down. I love anonymously tiptoeing into art openings for a free cheese cube and sip of wine, but I hate drifting through loud parties with little more to say than "Hey!" When's the last time you asked someone how their day was and expected more than a sentence in response? Do you know what pets your cronies from the local watering hole have at home? How about what your coworkers' favorite foods are? Slow down, sit down, and get down. Plan a powwow. Found the Crafty Lass Day Camp. Throw a sexy slumber party or rooftop romp. Here are some ideas for making getting primitive in the big city a group effort.

Powwow Power

Like campfires, powwows conjure up down-home nostalgia even in sophisticated circles. They're really just an excuse to dance, sing, and socialize, but they have more connective capability than a cocktail party. There's less flitting around and small talk and more handmade costumes and chanting. Read up on the traditions; borrow the ones that intrigue you and drop the ones that don't. Most powwows are dry affairs, but I would serve sangria. Some can go on for weeks, but most of us wouldn't be

Microcosmically primitive. All of these are small enough suggestions, but how about downright teensy prescriptions for an even quicker fix? Sleep naked. Open the windows (even when it's cold) and take a deep breath. Detour through the park and toss a few crumbs to the pigeons. Stalk the mysterious Miss Kitty and pounce like a feral friend. Make acorn art. Go a day without checking your look in the mirror. Let yourself get caught in a rainstorm. Keep a running list of your wild accomplishments to chart your little devolution. ❤️ able to stand that much togetherness. Up for getting on the mic? Powwows are often led by a master of ceremonies infamous for bad jokes. Design your powwow to suit your space and your tribe. Most of the details are up for grabs, but some practices are a must to keep your powwow from becoming a plain old party.

An outdoor space is ideal, but even a basement is an acceptable alternative. And if you don't have a yard or a spacious porch, lots of parks rent space for parties. Just make sure there's ample room for everyone to spread out in a circle. Circles are an integral part of a good powwow. One of the reasons campfires are so intimate is because circles are welcoming. There's always room—just widen the ring. Everyone meets face to face, and there's no chance to gravitate to a comfortable clique.

Keep the guest list small, but don't just invite the usual suspects. Mix it up. Bring in work friends and old college buddies. Ask everyone to dress in good floor-sitting garb. Avoid playing perfect hostess. Invest in some big coolers to keep drinks on hand. Put a lazy Susan in the middle of the circle so no one—not even you—has to get up for a refill. Fondue would make a great communal powwow meal. Worried about filling awkward dead air? Enlist a funny friend to help play MC. Have an idea potluck—ask everyone to bring a suggestion for

Big plans. These aren't just suggestions for fun gatherings; they're also perfect forums for planning a bona fide backcountry excursion. Invite a crew you'd like to camp with. Toss around trip plans. Share locale suggestions. Plan the menu. Before you know it you'll be roughing it for real. ❧

a group game. If all else fails, hot potato works in a pinch. But don't worry—powwow power is contagious. No one can resist its charm.

Crafty Counseling

Springtime on Staten Island in the eighties meant George Michael tunes pouring from open car windows and a flood of television commercials for Young People's Day Camp. The spot featured a smiling, talking yellow balloon and a kid who looked suspiciously like my neighbor. I suspected Little Anthony was running off to Young People's Day Camp for nonstop summer frolic while I was stuck jumping through the sprinkler in the driveway. I begged to go, but there was always some reason to miss registration.

At six I was traumatized by a pocket-sized book my mom received as a present. It was *The Book of Questions*, a collection of morally provocative queries, perfect for hell-raising around a powwow circle or campfire. My tiny heart was broken by a question that went something like: If your child was drowning and Jesus' voice boomed "Let her go! It is as it should be!" what would you do? Clearly Mom didn't realize the potential psychological damage of her answer, and at that age I didn't see yet how twelve years of Catholic school could mess with a mind. *The Book of Questions* comes in three flavors: original, business, and sexy. All are equally good for candid camaraderie and tantalizing dialogue in the wild or back at home. 🐾

Aside from the pressure of color wars, camp is a kid's dream. And why not? There's decoupage, picnic tables, and grass stains. It's not too late or too difficult to start a day camp right in your living room. Waive the pesky fees, get the girls together (boys are okay too), and write your own camp song. Borrow activities from the Scouts. Boy Scouts always get to hike all over the place, but the girls really hone their crafty indoor skills. Cover a frame in seashells. Bake sugar cookies shaped like deer. Crochet a forest. Learn knot tying while you make a set of nautical-themed Christmas tree ornaments. Line up your

Campy camp movies to motivate the troop:

Camp—Finally two great genres meet: the musical and the camp flick.

Camp Nowhere—Christopher Lloyd helps a group of spoiled kids invent a noncamp summer camp that includes video games instead of hikes. So bad but so good.

Indian Summer—perfect for a sentimental reunion, *Big Chill*-craving.

Meatballs—THE summer camp movie, complete with a young, irrepressible Bill Murray.

Sleepaway Camp—I was first scandalized by this twisted camp horror in seventh grade, and it still creeps me out today.

Wet Hot American Summer—a modern version of delicious B-movie camp mayhem.

White Water Summer—The kids don't actually go to camp, instead they're led around the wilderness by a mean, barely twenty Kevin Bacon, which is why this one made the list. 🐾

sleeping bags and cozy up to summer camp flicks for inspiration. Lead the gang on a nature hike in your local park. Fulfill dashed childhood dreams, complete with T-shirts emblazoned with your camp name. Kick off the season with a camping trip, and host the bittersweet end-of-season talent show back home in your living room.

Rustic Romance

I'm happy to say a trip to the backcountry guarantees good sex, but how about conjuring primal urges during dry spells in the city? In college a story circulated around campus about a couple who managed to make it to the roof of the administration building without tripping the alarm. Rumor was they snuck up in the middle of the night with nothing but a sleeping bag and a bottle of booze. They were found by a janitor in the morning, but they'd had their moment of romantic glory. For weeks this story occupied our lunch discussions and my imagination.

Sleeping on the floor aligns the spine and humbles the spirit. There's also something irrefutably exciting about not retreating

Primitive pairs. Take some cues from these notable wild couples. The obvious one—recreate original sin with fig-leaf bikinis. Dance by the light of the moon like the Owl and the Pussycat. Follow a spaghetti string to a coy kiss, à la Lady and the Tramp. Or just be Jane and let your Tarzan sweep you off your feet. Demand chest-banging to complete the fantasy. ❧

to your assigned bed. Add an attractive pal, and you've got the makings of a one-handed read. Camping provides a fresh, wild stage for our amorous animal acts. Back at home we may not be able to import the exhilarating fresh air or the thrilling landscape, but we can at least find a flat spot for a camp-inspired make-out session.

Start with a salacious email invite or lead a blindfolded guest by the hand to your surprise campsite. Head up to the roof. No roof access? Set up camp in the garden or on the fire escape, or just throw down on the bedroom floor. Go all out with the ambiance to recreate the backcountry experience, or keep it simple. Design a maze of plants with your love nest in the center. Buy a few bags of sand to roll around in. One thing's for sure—don't forget to pitch the tent. Improvise a lovers' lean-to with blankets, then cozy up in a sleeping bag. Set the mood with a recording of wild night sounds. Keep the lights low—bring a flashlight or a few candles. Turn scout games bad by playing without knickers. Frolic like bunnies or cuddle like two peas in a pod. Pack a picnic of sexy treats, but leave the utensils in the drawer. Toss each other grapes. Lick peanut butter off fingers. Sip whiskey from a canteen. When the sun comes up you'll be so hesitant to get back to reality you'll ignore the morning breath for hours, even though the electric toothbrush is just a few paces away.

For the Birds

Animal images are everywhere—notebooks, tote bags, T-shirts, jewelry. We pay constant homage to their cuteness with fabric, ink, and words, but how about a craft to actually serve them? Your camp's first order of business (after you decide on the uniforms) could be this tasty present—Feathered Chinatown Feeders. These Chinese take-out container bird feeders will be a flock hotspot. Hang them in a row outside your meeting room and pull up a seat for the peeping, tweeting, and fluttering. Who's flying in for the buffet? Pick up a native bird guide and make their acquaintance. Document your friends on film and piece together a panoramic collage for any room lacking a fowl view.

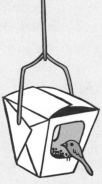

GATHER UP
Quart-sized Chinese take-out container
Pencil
Razor blade
Scissors
Card stock
Strong string or twine
Bird seed

1. Ask your favorite take-out joint for some free extra containers, or dump out the white rice as soon as you get home. A quick wipe down and dry out, and the container will look brand new. (Flip carefully when you decant the rice, and you'll make cool white rice castles too.)

2. Close up the container and pull the silver handle upright. Hold the container tightly, and rest the pencil under the handle in the center. Pull up gently on the pencil. The handle will easily bend to form a peak you can rest the string in later when you're ready to hang it up.

3. Using the pointy part of the razor, "drill" about ten small holes in the bottom, so moisture can escape.

4. Draw a doorway on the card stock. Make it about $2^1/_2$ inches long and $2^1/_2$ inches wide. Arches are traditional, but you could even do circles. I thought upside-down trapezoids worked for these, too. Now cut it out using the scissors.

5. Hold or tape the doorway to one of the plain (unfolded and handle-less) sides of the container. Place it $1^1/_2$ inches up from the bottom. Trace it. Repeat on the other plain side.

6. Using the razor, saw out the doorways. It's best to work with the container closed, and go slowly, so it doesn't tear.

7. Almost there. Tie a knot around the bend in the handle with about 12 inches of string. When you're ready to hang it up, make a loop at the top and trim the excess.

8. Don't forget to fill it with treats—homemade or store bought. Birds have different tastes—some like fruit, some like popcorn, and some like seeds. But a lot of birds like black-oil sunflower seeds. It's a sure bet, and a big bag is only $3.

TIPS

• I love looking out my window and seeing floating take-out containers. Their white, folded simplicity is what gets me, but feel free to add your own pizzazz to these. Paint, glue, or glitter them up. Just don't use anything birds might accidentally swallow.

• Hang these in winter when food is scarce, and you'll have chirping visitors all year round. But don't be discouraged if you hang them in warmer weather; it may take a while before the birds seek out your pit stop. Take advantage of a nearby tree; the safety of its branches may also encourage hungry customers.

• Don't forget to take these inside when it's raining, or refresh with new containers frequently. You don't want to treat your new friends to bird sludge.

Answer the Call

Bring nature home with a potted plant. Take time to appreciate small things. Say no to luxury once in a while. Treat buddies to more intimate gatherings. Pushing our bodies, paring down, disconnecting in order to be more connected—any steps we take to a more elemental appreciation of life are damn near applaudable. All these rustic rituals are fun and certainly worth adopting. They can be the baby steps on your path to nature girl. Give them a try when you need to quench your backcountry thirst between trips. They're utterly guileless, silly, nourishing goodness, but they are not the real deal. If they wield enough power to cleanse your crazies, you are way saner than me. Nothing slaps my reset button like camping. Ironically, the backcountry is the only place I've found where a girl can really get ready to conquer modern life (or just about anything that stands in her way). None of the try-this-at-home methods wash away the urban grit and tear down the city walls like a verifiable primitive excursion. From carrying a pack to designing camp, even in the scary spiders, warm cheese, and glorious post-camping shower—there are surprising possibilities, unique challenges, and near-perfect peace.

> **Is that a flashlight in your pack** or are you just happy to see me? When packing for your sexy sleepover, think feral—feathers and fur, tickle and tease. Think primal—essential oils and natural salves make for healing sensuous massages. And think practical—rope could come in handy even if there's not a food bag to hang. ❧

Head whole-hog into the backcountry. Spend some time doing nothing. Or do everything. Do it in the buff or in a strand of pearls. Camping is the original do-it-yourself, spontaneous, cheap, punk rock, mix and match, pure, and essential escape. Everything else is just a cover band, supermarket sushi, Robert Downey Jr. in any movie other than *Less Than Zero*. Get it? The wild is calling. Answer, damn it. No more dillydallying. Go on, get primitive!

Lessons from rocks. Recently I was killing gargantuan video-game spiders with a friend. Every chance he got, he went in, guns ablaze, and almost succeeded within an inch of his life. But when my turns were up, I was never very close to killing the things. I wasn't running in there, wand high, ready to sacrifice a few notches on the life meter to get the job done. I was holding back.

It is only a video game, but it reminded me of how the GLOK drove thirteen cramped hours in a borrowed Volkswagen to explore the Kentucky forest. On one of our hikes we found this great big boulder rumored to hide an unbelievable view. All we had to do was scale the steep side of it. And I simply couldn't. I stood wide-eyed and motionless while Rachel shimmied her way up. The climb seemed so steep, so insurmountable. I thought if I tried, I would just fall back down. I probably would have if I'd held back. Or maybe I could have made it with a bold running start. During the long car ride back home I promised myself that the next time I would find out. Whether it's a big climb or animated spiders, I decided, next time I won't walk away not knowing. That's why I love camping—nothing else dares me quite so much to see what happens when I run in with my wand held high. ❧

Resources

As promised, here are links, links, and more links. Plan your trip, buy a tent, talk to fellow campers, and seek out swimming holes—all online.

Trip Planning

www.americantrails.org	American Trails
www.appalachiantrail.org	Appalachian Trail Conservancy
www.backcountry.net	National scenic trails mailing list
www.blm.gov	Bureau of Land Management
www.fs.fed.us	U.S. National Forest Service
www.nps.gov	U.S. National Park Service
www.pcta.org	Pacific Crest Trail Association
www.recreation.gov	Information on recreation on all federal public lands
www.reserveamerica.com	Information about and reservation of campgrounds

Gearing Up

www.backcountry.com	Backcountry.com
www.campmor.com	Campmor
www.coleman.com	Coleman
www.ems.com	EMS
www.outdoordivas.com	Outdoor Divas—gear for women
www.outdoorgearswap.com	Mountain Equipment Co-op
www.rei.com	REI

Outdoor Magazines and Forums

www.backpacker.com	*Backpacker* magazine
www.gorp.com	GORP, also part of *Outside*
www.outside.away.com	*Outside* magazine
www.thebackpacker.com	*The Backpacker*—a small online magazine

Conservation

www.lnt.org	Leave No Trace Center for Outdoor Ethics
www.treadlightly.org	Tread Lightly! Ethics

Other Fun Stuff

www.byways.org	America's Byways
www.maryjanesfarm.com	MaryJanesFarm—camping food, farm classes, and farm vacations

Other Fun Stuff, continued

www.nwf.org   National Wildlife Federation

www.rayjardine.com   Ray Jardine's Adventure Page—
                               the famous camper's instruc-
                               tions and supplies for making
                               your own gear

www.scoutorama.com   Scoutorama—all things scout

www.swimmingholes.org   Swimming Holes.info—insider's
                               guide to America's secret swimming
                               spots

www.worldwildlife.org   World Wildlife Fund

Further Reading

Here are some of the handy big hitters and old standards of back-country literature.

The Ashley Book of Knots by Clifford Ashley (Doubleday, 1944)

The Backpacker's Handbook by Chris Townsend
(International Marine/Ragged Mountain Press, 2004)

Backpacking: A Woman's Guide by Adrienne Hall
(International Marine/Ragged Mountain Press, 1998)

Basic Wilderness Survival Skills by Bradford Angier;
Lamar Underwood (Editor) (The Lyons Press, 2002)

Beyond Backpacking: Ray Jardine's Guide to Lightweight Hiking by
Ray Jardine (Adventurelore Press, 1999)

Boy Scouts of America: The Official Handbook for Boys by
Boy Scouts of America (Applewood Books, 1997)

Campfire Cuisine: Gourmet Recipes for the Great Outdoors by Robin
Donovan (Quirk Books, 2006)

Campfire Songs by Irene Maddox (Editor) (Globe Pequot, 1998)

The Complete Book of Knots by Geoffrey Budworth
(The Lyons Press, 1997)

Games for Girl Scouts by Girl Scouts of United States of America (Prentice Hall, 1990)

Handbook of Nature Study by Anna Botsford Comstock, Verne N. Rockcastle (Comstock Publishing, 1986)

Hiking and Backpacking: Essential Skills to Advanced Techniques by Victoria Logue (Menasha Ridge Press, 2005)

Identifying and Harvesting Edible and Medicinal Plants in Wild (and Not So Wild) Places by Steve Brill (Harper Paperbacks, 1994)

National Geographic Guide to the State Parks of the United States by National Geographic Society (National Geographic, 2004)

National Geographic Guide to the National Parks of the United States by National Geographic Society (National Geographic, 2003)

Tree Finder: A Manual for the Identification of Trees by Their Leaves by May T. Watts (Nature Study Guild Publishers, 1991)

The Wild Muir: Twenty-Two of John Muir's Greatest Adventures by John Muir, Lee Stetson, Yosemite Association (Yosemite Association, 1994)

About the Author

Heather Menicucci is a writer, film-maker, and unabashed dabbler with an impressive sticker collection. She has produced award-winning short films, reported on National Park Service meetings, contributed to *BUST* magazine, and filmed epic sweet-sixteen galas. Although she dreams of someday permanently pitching her tent in Costa Rica, she currently makes camp in New York and Pennsylvania. Next up on her backcountry agenda: learn to fish. Visit Heather at www.letsgetprimitive.com.

Index